THE
LATE VICTO
TOWN

Frank Grace

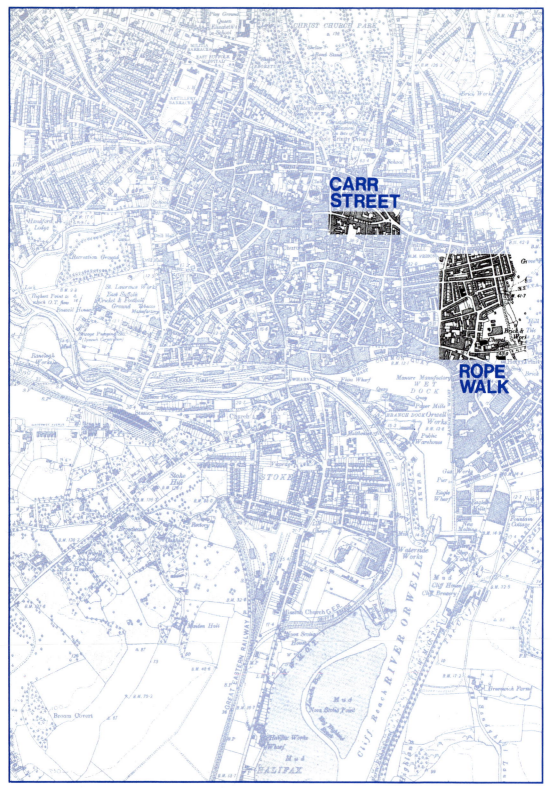

1. Part of an Ordnance Survey map, six inches to one mile, 1902-3. This identifies the two sites used in the text, both in the Suffolk town of Ipswich. They are Carr Street, a central shopping street, and the Rope Walk area to the east of the town, close to the docks and a major iron foundry.

Learning Local History 2
General Editor: David Dymond

THE
LATE VICTORIAN
TOWN

Frank Grace

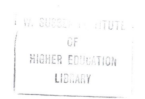
Published by PHILLIMORE for
BRITISH ASSOCIATION FOR LOCAL HISTORY
with the aid of a grant from the
Calouste Gulbenkian Foundation

1992

Published for
BRITISH ASSOCIATION FOR LOCAL HISTORY

by
PHILLIMORE & CO. LTD.
Shopwyke Hall, Chichester, Sussex

ISBN 0 85033 712 7

Printed and bound in Great Britain by
STAPLES PRINTERS ROCHESTER LIMITED
Neptune Close, Medway City Estate, Frindsbury, Rochester, Kent.

Contents

List of Illustrations and Documents vii
Acknowledgements ix

Introduction xi

I Setting up the Assignment 1

    Town Plans 5
    Censuses 11
    Street Directories 13
    Poor-rate Books 16

II Organising the Work: Initial Decisions 17

III Study Area 1: A Working-class District 19

    Household Size 21
    Age Structure 21
    Birthplaces 23
    Occupations 27
    Housing 32
    Public Health 37
    'Biographies' 41
    Vice and Virtue 42
    Poverty 43

IV Study Area 2: A Central Shopping Street 44

    The Street in 1881: Finding our Whereabouts 46
    Nos. 5-9 Carr Street 48
    The Co-op Store 49
    Reminiscences 51
    Advertisements 56
    Continuity and Change in a Shopping Street 57
    Architecture in the Street: A Changing Townscape 59

V The Young Historian 67

    Select Bibliography 69
    Index 71

List of Illustrations and Documents

1.	Ipswich, showing the two study areas	ii
2.	Old properties in Fore Street, Ipswich	2
3.	The south side of Carr Street, Ipswich	2
4.	Seventeenth-century house, Rope Walk area	4
5.	The second premises of the Ipswich Co-operative Society, 1875-86	4
6.	Detail of John Ogilby's map of Ipswich, 1674	6
7.	Detail of Joseph Pennington's map of Ipswich, 1778	6
8.	A reconstructed map showing the Rope Walk area in 1841	7
9.	Detail of Edward White's map of Ipswich, 1849	7
10.	Detail of an Ordnance Survey map, 1925	8
11.	Detail of an Ordnance Survey map, 1924-5, with additions in 1938	8
12.	Detail of the town plan of Ipswich, 1881	9
13.	Page from an enumerator's book of 1851	10
14.	Extract from the Registrar General's instructions to enumerators, 1851	12
15.	Extract from a directory of Ipswich, 1881	14
16.	Extract from a poor-rate book, 1881	15
17.	Index card for recording households in census returns	18
18.	Detail of the town plan of Ipswich, 1881	20
19.	A simple form for tabulating ages in five-year groups	22
20.	Age structure expressed as a bar chart	22
21.	Birthplaces shown by pie chart	22
22.	Extract from the autobiography of Thomas Wood, Engineer	24
23.	Extract from an enumerator's book, 1881	25
24.	Extract from K. Chesney, *The Victorian Underworld*	26
25.	Extract from John Glyde, *The Moral, Social and Religious Condition of Ipswich*	27
26.	Extract from Henry Mayhew, *London Labour and the London Poor*	28
27.	Sample of a census abstract	30
28.	Extract from M. Llewellyn Davies, *Maternity: Letters from Working Women*	31
29.	Detail of the town plan of Ipswich, 1881	33
30.	Detail of the town plan of Ipswich, 1881	33
31.	Transcript of a census enumerator's book, 1881	35
32.	Transcript of a rate book, 1881, east side of Long Lane	36
33.	Extract from an annual sanitary report, 1874	37
34.	Extract from an annual sanitary report, 1889	38/39
35.	Contemporary description of insanitary courts, 1850	40
36.	Contemporary description of an urban family	40
37.	Detail of the town plan of Ipswich, 1881	45
38.	Extract from a directory, 1881	47

39.   Details extracted from a census enumerator's book, 1881 48
40.   Transcript of a rate book, 1881 49
41.   Architect's drawing of a new Co-op store, 1886 50
42.   Contemporary description of a new store, 1886 50
43.   An example of recorded reminiscences 52
44.   Contemporary description of a street trade 53
45.   Advertisement from an illustrated guide to Ipswich, 1890 54
46.   Advertisement from an almanack, 1890 54
47.   Advertisement from an almanack, 1890 55
48.   Advertisement from a directory, 1926 55
49.   Advertisement from a directory, 1910 56
50.   Extract from a directory, 1939 58
51.   Junction of Carr Street and Upper Brook Street, 1881 60
52.   Timber-framed building at the corner of Cox Lane and Carr Street 61
53.   Newspaper article about the demolition of an old building 61
54.   Junction of Carr Street and Upper Brook Street, 1890 62
55.   Extract from a guidebook, 1890 62
56.   Development plan, 1887 63
57.   Extract from a directory during redevelopment, 1890 64
58.   Photographic panorama of Carr Street, 1928 65
59.   Shopping centre plan, 1973 66
60.   Modern photograph of Carr Street 66

Acknowledgements

In preparing this book, I have luckily had the help of staff in the Suffolk Record Office, the most friendly of places in which to work. Clive Paine, the Advisory Teacher for Archives, who first put the idea to me, has shown an enthusiasm that has been particularly encouraging. David Dymond, as General Editor, has been as constructive in his criticisms as he has been unstinting of his time in helping to shape the book in its later stages. My thanks are due to them as colleagues and friends who helped when I stumbled.

Extracts from the enumerators' books for St Margaret's parish, Ipswich [Documents **13** and **14**], are reproduced by permission of the Public Record Office, Office of Population and Censuses, Crown Copyright. The extract from the autobiography of Thomas Wood [**23**] from J. Burnett, *Useful Toil*, is reproduced by permission of Allen Lane, Ltd.; that from K. Chesney, *The Victorian Underworld* [**24**], by permission of Maurice Temple Smith; the extracts from M. L. Davies, *Maternity: Letters from Working Women* [**28**], by permission of Virago Press; all other illustrations are reproduced by kind permission of the Suffolk Record Office. The photographs of contemporary Ipswich [**2**, **3** and **61**] were provided by the author.

NOTE: The bold numbers in square brackets, thus [**12**], refer to documents which are distributed throughout the text. They consist of extracts from manuscript sources and printed works, as well as maps, drawings, engravings and photographs.

INTRODUCTION

This book offers practical guidance to history teachers in schools, particularly those facing the challenge of organising groupwork on local topics and primary sources. It also discusses the motivation and experience of the pupils themselves — the 'young historians' who are following syllabuses leading to the General Certificate of Secondary Education (G.C.S.E.). We further hope that the approach and methods offered here may prove useful to those pursuing local history in other ways: for example at Advanced Level, in Adult Education, in local societies and research groups, and, indeed, as individual researchers.

What follows is based on the belief that the concepts of locality, neighbourhood and community are educationally stimulating, and that they must always be related to the wider themes and background of national history. In this sense our motives are similar to those behind the project known as 'History Around Us', successfully pursued for more than a decade and now part of the Schools History Project. Pupils working with local primary sources begin to 'Do History' for themselves and do not merely have it done to them; they learn to think historically, and not just to remember and regurgitate. By demonstrating constantly that the teaching of history and the learning of historical skills are indissolubly linked, this book has another unashamed and passionate purpose: to anathematise the sterile debate now raging about the teaching of history, often summarised as 'Skills versus Content'. If ever there was a false dichotomy, this is surely it!

The introduction of the G.C.S.E. and the publication of a National Curriculum for history are having, and will continue to have, fundamental effects on the teaching of history in schools and on the learning processes of pupils. The criteria laid down for the examination nationally require pupils to be involved in a range of activities, particularly in assignments based on primary sources. The emphasis is on pupils beginning to understand the nature of historical research, and acquiring the skills needed to handle different kinds of source, primary, secondary, statistical and visual. For its part, the final report of the National Curriculum History Working Group, published in April 1990, clearly approves the 'well-developed tradition of studying local history in school', and stresses the value in any history syllabus of 'taking the locality and its community as a comprehensive field for study'. It argues that local history should support all its Study Units, both those in the core and those which are optional, and further demands that some units designed by the schools themselves 'must be devoted specifically to local history' and used in the context of British social history. Disturbingly, however, most of the opportunities to study local history and local primary sources seem confined to the younger age-groups. Children aged from 11 to 16 have distinctly fewer chances of this kind of experience because their part of the curriculum swings strongly towards European and world history.

The methods and sources discussed in this book are not meant to be prescriptive and final; they merely suggest approaches to the study of the late Victorian town which a practising teacher has found workable with young historians. The tasks involved probably have a range greater than the G.C.S.E. actually requires, but they can be used selectively and adapted as a means of defining worthwhile assignments and fulfilling the requirements of different examining boards. Of course, the challenge of new examinations and a new curriculum is not only felt in the classroom. It takes time to organise projects capable of interesting groups and whole classes, so the following pages deliberately address the teacher's practical and logistical problems in preparing for such work and using precious time to best advantage.

The practical aims of this book are to:

1) Suggest ways in which teachers can, in the classroom, set and organise projects based on local sources.
2) Offer guidance on the availability of documentary sources, and on how to gain access to them.
3) Discuss the nature and origins of chosen sources.
4) Suggest ways in which students can be encouraged to handle historical evidence in a disciplined way: to transcribe, extract, analyse and interpret evidence.
5) Suggest ways in which assignments using local sources can be related to topics within the wider historical context of social and economic history.

The educational objectives of this guide are to:

1) Encourage students to enjoy the detective work of history: taking a critical approach to historical evidence, and testing its reliability; distinguishing between historical 'fact' and the suppositions or inferences which historians make in their work.
2) Help students to understand the important concepts of change and continuity, which are present in all forms of history.
3) Encourage students, when they are studying historical individuals and communities, to combine a critical approach to the past with imagination and sympathy, and to develop ideas about the ways in which people acted, thought and felt in the past, based upon historical evidence (often known as empathy).
4) Give students a grounding in the statistical analysis of historical data, and in the interpretation of statistics.
5) Help students to understand the language of historical writing: to distinguish between statements like 'it is probable', 'the evidence suggests', 'there is strong supporting evidence' and 'it must have been'.
6) Encourage students to present their findings and conclusions in a clear, logical manner so that they can be understood by those unfamiliar with the subject.

The two themes explored here relate to the study of the late 19th-century town or city, and focus on:

1) The study of a working-class district.
2) The study of a central shopping street.

This book constantly stresses the need to relate work done on local sources to major topics of national history, and in particular to those found in syllabuses covering the social and economic history of the 19th and 20th centuries. Thus, at different points in the text, the following general topics are referred to:

Architectural styles (especially Victorian)
Urban growth
Housing conditions, housing legislation and slum clearance
Social change: family planning, health and life expectancy
Migration: migrant labour and lodging-houses
Women and work
Social investigators: Henry Mayhew, Charles Booth, Seebohm Rowntree
The Co-operative Movement
Shops and shopping: the Retailing Revolution and street trades.

The specific examples which are used in this book come from the town of Ipswich, in Suffolk, during the 1880s, and are taken from two distinct areas within it. One is a district of working-class housing (known as the Rope Walk area) which came into existence in the 1840s; the other is a main shopping street in the centre of the town called Carr Street [1].

In examining these two very different areas and communities, four key sources are used which are likely to be available for most large towns. They are:

Town Plans published by the Ordnance Survey at large scale (that covering
    Ipswich was surveyed in 1881 and published in 1883-4)
Enumerators' Books from the census of 1881
Street Directories (in this case, Steven's *Directory of Ipswich*, 1881)
Poor-rate Books

Below you will find an explanation of the origins and uses of these sources (and of other sources normally accessible which could be used to expand the work). The key sources are equally applicable and fundamental to other kinds of project, and to other historical periods: for example you could use them to study an élite middle-class suburb, or a quarter developed for artisans. They could also be used to study one area or street over several decades.

The town, Ipswich, and the sources have been chosen because they are representative and can be paralleled elsewhere. Though never a major industrial centre, Ipswich nonetheless reflects, in its history, the social and economic changes consequent upon the Industrial Revolution: its rapid population growth from about eleven thousand inhabitants in 1811 to over 50,000 in 1881; the development of its industries, port and docks; the physical expansion of its housing areas; the transformation of its medieval core by the erection of new public and commercial buildings.

By the late 19th century, similar developments can be seen all over the country. By 1881 urban society was the norm in England and Wales, for over 50 per cent of the population then lived in towns of over 20,000 people. Ipswich approximates to the experience of towns as different economically as Rochdale, Wigan, Derby, Exeter and Tynemouth. The year 1881 is probably a better choice than earlier dates because, not only is the census taken in that year available for study, but by then street directories and town plans are much more likely to exist, and as a further bonus early photographs are likely to have survived as well.

Thus, for a major period of history about a century ago, the existence of good sources encourages us to focus on a locality at a particular point in time. It also enables us to raise major questions about urban society in general. How does area X or street Y throw light on the general processes of historical change? This relationship between the general and particular lies at the heart of all historical research. The local study must then be seen in a wider context, which in this case is the framework of a broad syllabus. What follows will therefore stress these interrelated concerns in order to demonstrate how young historians can engage in real and valuable historical enquiry, and in the process can acquire some of the skills of the professional historian.

I

SETTING UP THE ASSIGNMENT

First of all, it will be necessary to locate the required documentary and other sources, as well as secondary material on the history of the town. It will undoubtedly take some time to prepare a 'pack' for classroom use, and the job may be best done by a team of teachers. The first point of contact is the local Reference Library or, in some boroughs, the Local History Library. The assistants here should be able to give you preliminary advice on published histories of the town, local journals, newspapers, photographic collections and the like. For primary documentary or archival evidence, the main depository will be the County Record Office. Once relevant documents have been located in catalogues, it will probably be best to sample them quickly. Census returns, for instance, may well be on microfilm and, given that a potential street or area has been chosen, it will be necessary to see whether the copy is a good one and the handwriting sufficiently clear and legible for use in the classroom. If it is not, then a transcript will be needed.

It might also be worthwhile to contact local history societies, family history societies and research groups in your town or area. An approach to the secretary could lead to discussions with researchers already at work in the field, and already very knowledgeable. It might even be possible to establish a link between the society and the school whereby, for example, local historians could be invited to talk to the class or to lead them on an excursion. Such contacts will broaden the educational context of the project, and emphasise its relevance to the local community. This, the social importance of historical studies, cannot be over-stressed, and we should seize any opportunity of showing that history can stimulate and unite people. For example, the school may already have a programme of community service which involves helping the elderly. Old people are usually very willing to talk about their experiences, and their memories are vital historical evidence of a neighbourhood or community before it was socially transformed or slum-cleared. Here is an excellent channel for the young to meet the old, to ask them questions and record their memories. In this way, our students are learning the techniques of the oral historian, carefully framing questions which will elicit significant information, transcribing taped interviews and editing the results.

In choosing a precise street or neighbourhood for study, teachers will in all probability be influenced by its proximity to the school, or by its familiarity to students. The visual evidence of standing buildings need not be over-emphasised as a prerequisite, because old working-class districts have often been cleared as slums, while central shopping streets have inevitably been modernised or 'comprehensively' developed in the post-war period. If, however, some earlier buildings have survived, they will indeed be worth investigating.

2. **The architectural record**: old properties in Fore Street, Ipswich, on the south side of the Rope Walk area (photographed in 1987). Note particularly the brick frontages: the one on the right with its parapet is clearly added to the original structure. The interiors of all of these buildings are of the 16th century. They were part of the old merchant quarter until the end of the 18th century. This site shows the constantly changing nature of street frontages. Since 1987 this whole block has been both renovated and redeveloped.

3. **Architectural mixtures**: a photograph of 1989 showing the south side of Carr Street, Ipswich. On the right is part of Woolworth's store, established in the mid-1920s. In the centre are the only timber-framed buildings remaining in the street today, housing Currys and Dewhurst; the latter is heavily disguised by a later frontage. Note their scale compared to the Victorian and 20th-century structures on either side. On the left is a range of buildings belonging to the Co-operative Society, with four different frontages dating, right to left, from 1885-6, 1908 (with date plaque), 1928 and 1915. Notice how these are all masked at ground-floor level by modern shop-fronts.

For example, the Rope Walk area of Ipswich was cleared in the 1930s, but houses, some from the 17th century with decayed 19th-century frontages, are still to be seen [2]. Other surviving features include part of an elementary school which served the locality, a few lines of old kerbstones in 'Long Street' and a large white-brick workshop. Carr Street, also, though transformed by a brutal shopping precinct of the 1960s, still offers a varied and historically interesting set of buildings, including a Co-op store of 1885, parts of 'improvements' made in the late 1880s, and some earlier survivals [3]. All these features can be profitably recorded on a first visit to the site. Visual evidence of this kind may not in itself be very exciting, but it can help students to appreciate that all historical evidence is fragmentary and incomplete. To counteract the losses, it should be possible to find prints or photographs in a local record office, library or museum which will depict buildings now demolished or radically transformed [4 & 5]. Such evidence often exists for the main streets of towns, and it will provide an instructive comparison with the same site or building today.

If you decide to visit the site with a class, it would be advisable to arrange a preliminary session in the classroom or library to discuss the variety of Victorian and 20th-century architectural styles. This might provide the opportunity for liaison with the art department of your school. On site, students should make a detailed sketch-plan of the street and take careful notes. If the site is a shopping street, they should record:

1) Each building whether shop, house or pub, in sequence along each side.
2) The style of each building (this should be done by a combination of written notes, drawings and still or video photography).
3) Particular features, especially date plaques, building materials, roof lines and ornamentation.
4) The relationship between shops and their surroundings (e.g. two or more shops may be inserted into one large earlier building). Students *must* learn to look above ground-floor level!
5) The widths of frontages, whether of shops or houses, so that they can be compared with maps or plans of earlier date.

Having visited the site and recorded evidence on the ground, the class can then be introduced to maps and plans. These are essential for any detailed work on the urban environment. The main purpose, at this stage, is to look for evidence of physical change over a period of time. At Ipswich, for example, we have a map of 1674 by John Ogilby and a very fine map of 1778 by Joseph Pennington. In the 19th century Edward White produced maps in 1849 and 1867. The Ordnance Survey, set up in 1792, began to publish its large-scale maps (25 inches to the mile) from 1854, and these were later revised. Thus, the Ipswich survey of 1881 was published in 1883-4 and updated in 1905 and later.

A similar range of maps is available for most towns. Photocopied extracts can be obtained for the chosen area of study, and assembled in chronological sequence [6-11]. This will enable students to identify the main changes in the townscape, and to date them at least approximately. For example, the Ipswich sequence clearly indicates that

4. An architectural print: a house of the mid-17th century in New Street, Ipswich, in the Rope Walk area. Taken from *Views of Old Ipswich*, p. 23, by Edward Pococke, a local artist of the mid-19th century. The overhanging bressummer at first-floor level, the doorway on the left and the roof-line are all typical of the period. Note the decayed plasterwork. Old houses like this deteriorated as the surrounding area filled up with working-class housing, and by the 1880s were reported by the Medical Officer of Health as being insanitary and overcrowded.

5. An architectural drawing: the second premises of the Ipswich Co-operative Society, 1875-86. Taken from *Through Sixty Years; A Record of Progress and Achievement prepared on the Occasion of the Diamond Jubilee* (1928), p. 18. The Society started its life in Carr Street, in a house to the the right of that shown here. Notice the signboard which mentions the date of the Society's foundation. This building was formerly the *Wellington Inn*: note the entrance to the old inn-yard, the bricked-up windows on the second floor and the style of the Victorian shop-front.

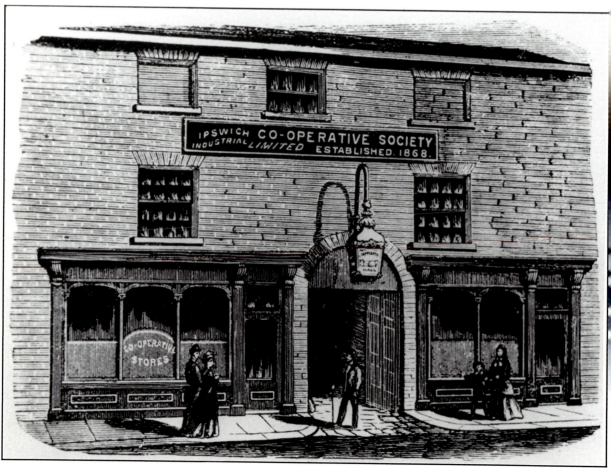

the Rope Walk area was transformed in the period between 1841 and 1849, when large numbers of working-class houses were built, and, more recently, Ordnance Survey maps of 1925 and 1938 pinpoint when slum clearance took place.

Town plans

The most useful and fascinating maps of all, however, are the town plans that were produced between 1843 and 1894. These are at very large scales, of which 1:500 or 10.56 feet to one mile is typical. That for Ipswich was surveyed in 1881, and a sample from the Rope Walk area is given [12]. Such plans were drawn for all towns with more than 4,000 inhabitants, and should be available in local record offices. They provide information about:

> The names of streets and courts.
> The layout of houses, outbuildings, sheds, glasshouses, etc.
> The location of important industrial sites, schools, churches, chapels, public houses, etc.
> The different types of housing: terraces, back-to-back houses, semi-detached, detached villas, etc.; those houses which had front areas, or rear access, or access to the rear by tunnel. They even give some indication of steps up to front doors, and show paths and trees in back gardens and yards. Street furniture such as letter-boxes, lamp-posts, lamp brackets and manhole covers (evidence of main drains).

Even more important for the study of housing conditions, the plans allow us to measure accurately the ground-plans of houses and the widths of lanes, alleys, courts and backyards, and the shape of outbuildings and industrial sites. Short Lane in Ipswich was, for example, only nine feet wide and about two hundred feet long, and yet it housed over 100 people. The cottages at the north-east end of Long Lane were 20 by 15 feet, while those in Trinity Square were only 15 by 12 feet [18].

The initial exploration of the site and maps provides a context, both visual and temporal, within which a deeper study based on census returns and other sources can later be fitted. At this early stage, it will be important to discuss with the class topics relevant to the general syllabus: urban growth in the 19th century, housing conditions and slum-clearance in the 20th century, shops and shopping, and the general history of the town itself. As an urban study develops, town plans will be referred to constantly as a way of understanding the physical environment in which varied groups of inhabitants lived.

Once the areas for study have been selected, and background work done, students can be introduced to the key documentary sources on which so much of their work will rest. The teacher has the difficult task of introducing these, while still leaving students an opportunity to think for themselves how useful and reliable such sources are, and how best they can be exploited.

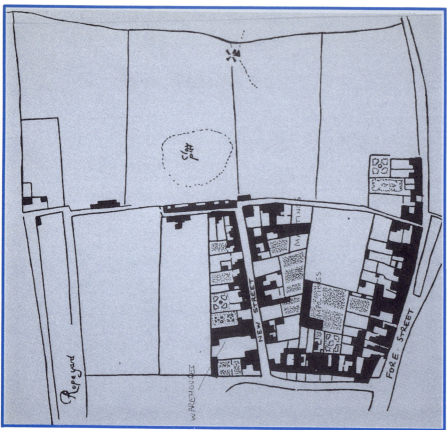

7. Part of Joseph Pennington's map of Ipswich, 1778. A century or more after the development of New Street, the area was little changed, except for maltings and warehouses built over some of the back gardens.

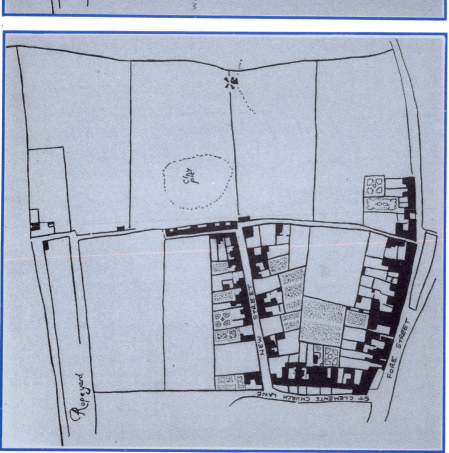

6. Part of John Ogilby's map of Ipswich, 1674. New Street came into existence in the early 17th century as an extension to the older merchant quarter of Fore Street, adjacent to the river. Note the formal layout of the gardens. To the north and east were rural fields, except for two 'industrial' sites called the 'Clay Pit' and 'Ropeyard'. The latter name was subsequently adopted for the area as a whole, and the former name probably explains why the area was alternatively known as 'The Potteries'.

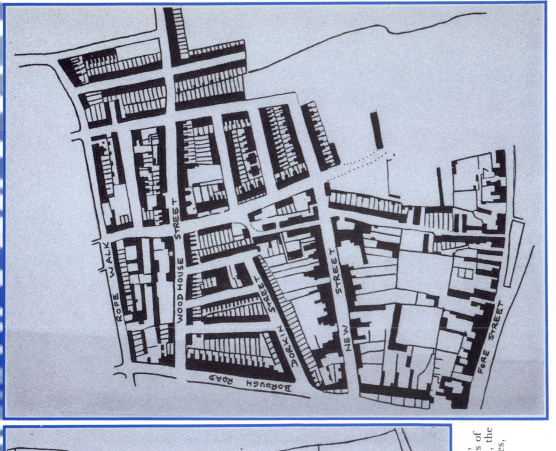

8. (*Above*) **A reconstructed map showing the Rope Walk area in 1841**, based on the census of 1841 and Pennington's map of 1778. The beginnings of major change are now apparent. Long Lane is lined with terraced cottages, the north-west corner of the site is being laid out with streets of workers' houses, and the old Rope Yard is being infilled.

9. (*Right*) **Part of Edward White's map of Ipswich, 1849.** The transformation of the Rope Walk area is virtually complete. This map confirms the 1840s as the crucial decade of economic and social change in Ipswich as a whole, with the building of the new wet dock, the emergence of Ransome's ironworks as a major industrial enterprise, the arrival of the railway in 1846, and the greatest growth of population in the 19th century.

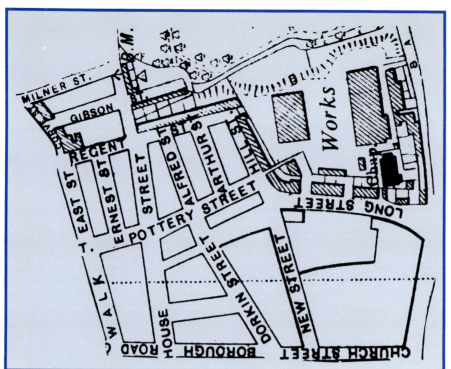

11. Part of an Ordnance Survey map, six inches to one mile, enlarged, 1924-5, with additions in 1938. Virtually all the houses of the 1840s have been slum-cleared, following the Housing Act of 1935 and a public enquiry in the town, leaving only a skeleton of the streets themselves. By 1939 the former inhabitants had all been moved to new council housing on the east of the town. The Rope Walk area was to remain derelict until the 1950s, since when it has become the site of a College of Higher and Further Education.

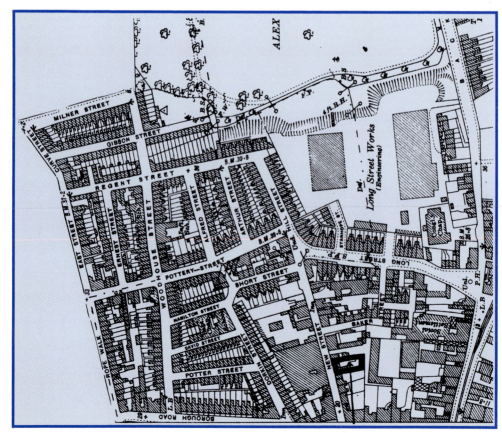

10. Part of an Ordnance Survey map, 25 inches to one mile, reduced, 1925. A number of changes have occurred since the mid-19th century. Long Lane, now Long Street, has been widened, and much of its housing rebuilt as a result of the work of the Medical Officer of Health. Some notorious courts off Fore Street have been replaced by the Social Settlement, the work of a local philanthropist; the Long Street Works has appeared in the south-east corner — a munitions factory of the First World War. Otherwise, the physical appearance of the area is little changed.

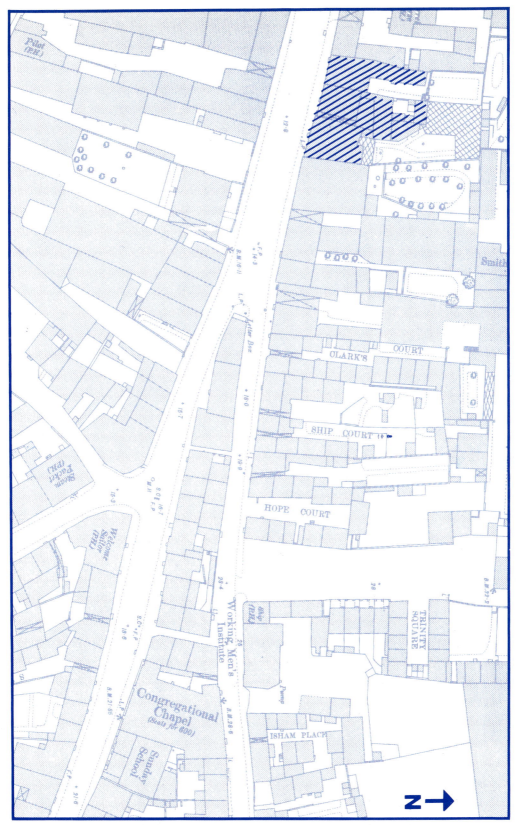

12. Part of the town plan of Ipswich, 10.56 feet to one mile, 1881, showing the south side of the Rope Walk area. The shaded section indicates the site of the old buildings on Fore Street [2].

13. Sample page from an enumerator's book of 1851, with the entries for Nos. 5-21 Carr Street, Ipswich. Note the short diagonal lines under some names in column five, meant to separate houses and their occupants but not strictly conforming to Direction Three of the 'General Instruction to the Enumerator'. Note also that Nos. 7, 11 and 17 are entered as uninhabited (column four); in fact No. 17 was the premises of the *East Anglian Daily Times*, a local newspaper. The census therefore does not reliably inform us whether a building, particularly a shop or office, was, or was not, in commercial use.

Censuses

Students will need to know the following background information. The first official census was taken in March 1801, and with one exception (1941, during the Second World War) censuses have been taken at ten-yearly intervals ever since. The censuses of 1801, 1811, 1821 and 1831 were all statistical, and gave no information about named individuals: they did, however, give the total numbers of individuals or families in various occupational groups, and the number of houses inhabited and uninhabited (from 1811 also the number of houses being built). The early censuses were organised by the Overseers of the Poor for each parish. In 1841 a newly created Registrar General's Office decided to ask for more detail and therefore reorganised the system. From that date, individual schedules (forms) were distributed to each household by Enumerators. The latter were appointed by the Registrars of new Registration Districts which were carved out of the Poor Law Unions of 1834. The information now asked for was much more precise: the name of each member of the household, his or her age, occupation and place of origin (whether in the county or not). When the schedules had been collected house by house, they were then copied into enumerators' books [13], which were in turn sent by the local registrar to the Registrar General in London.

In 1851 yet more exact information was required. Now each individual had to be defined in terms of relationship to the head of household, marital condition (married, unmarried, widow or widower), and the actual parish of birth. By this date, too, the enumerators' books had to provide a description of the route or area covered by each enumerator, and a statistical summary of the main entries. The basic format of the returns remains the same for decades, though, under the terms of the 100-year rule, we shall not be able to examine the enumerators' books for 1891 until 1992. Printed Abstracts and statistical tables for each census down to 1981 are available in most reference libraries, however, and are particularly useful for studying broad demographic trends and the occupational structure of large towns [27].

In addition to samples of the enumerators' books, it will be very useful to have the Registrar General's instructions (or the 'Directions respecting the manner of entering the Schedules') [14]. These describe the way in which each house, and each family within a house, was to be distinguished, and the different abbreviations or 'contractions' that were to be used by enumerators. Copies of the census can then be issued to students, and in groups they should be able quickly to familiarise themselves with the vital technicalities.

In spite of the difficulties involved, students should, if possible, be confronted with a facsimile rather than a typed transcript, so that they can appreciate that this evidence, like any other historical source, has to be looked at critically because *it is imperfect*. A number of such points may arise immediately the documents are examined:

The enumerator may have had poor handwriting, which is not easily legible.
He may have made some obvious mistakes.
Entries may be scored through with pencil or crayon.

GENERAL INSTRUCTION TO THE ENUMERATOR.

As soon as possible after the completion of the Enumeration—

(1.) *Arrange the Householders' Schedules and other Schedules in order* so that all those relating to one Parish or Township, Hamlet, or other Local Sub-division, are **together.**

(2.) COPY VERY LEGIBLY *in ink* the Schedules into this *Enumeration Book*, in accordance with the following directions:—

Directions respecting the manner of entering the Schedules.

1. Insert first, in the spaces at the top of the page, the name of the Civil Parish, or Township, City or Municipal Borough, Ward (if in a City or Municipal Borough), Parliamentary Borough, Town, Village, &c., Urban Sanitary District, Rural Sanitary District, and Ecclesiastical Parish or District in which the houses of that page are situate.

2. In the first column, write the *No.* of the *Schedule* you are about to copy, commencing with No. 1: in the second column the name of the Road, Street, Square, &c., where the house is situate, and the No. of the *house*, or any distinctive name by which it is known; then insert in the third column the figure 1 for an inhabited House, and Copy from the Schedule into the other columns all the particulars concerning the persons mentioned therein, making use of any of the authorized contractions (see below), and taking especial care to class the *ages* of MALES and FEMALES *under* their PROPER COLUMNS.

Enter in the same manner the other Schedules, up to the last, in strict numerical order.

3. Under the name of the last entered person in each *house* draw a strong DOUBLE line, as in the example on the opposite page, to separate the inmates from those of the house next following; and where there is *more than one Occupier* in the same house, draw a *single* line to distinguish each Family, as in the example. [NOTE.—A Lodger, *with or without a family, is to be considered an Occupier.*]

4. If you have enumerated any persons in Canal Boats or Barges, enter the *Schedules for Vessels* in the same manner as the Householders' Schedules, stating in col. 2 the locality in which the boats, &c., were met with.

5. Where you have to insert an uninhabited house, or a house building, do this by writing in the fourth column, "1 U," or "1 B," on a distinct line, taking care to omit none which are noted in your Memorandum Book. When two or more houses uninhabited or building, occur together, insert the total number, thus:—"3 U," "2 B," as the case may be.

6. At the bottom of each **page**, on the line for that purpose, enter the total *number* of HOUSES in that page, as in the example. If the statement respecting any inhabited house is continued from one page to another, that house will be reckoned in the total of the houses in the page on which the *first* name is entered. Enter also, on the line at the foot of the page, the total number of MALES and FEMALES in that page.

7. When all the Schedules belonging to any one *Civil Parish or Township, Borough, Ward, Town, Village, Hamlet, Urban Sanitary District, Rural Sanitary District, or Ecclesiastical Parish or District,* have been entered, write across the page, "*End of the Civil Parish [or Township] of*———," "*End of the Borough, Ward, Town, Hamlet, &c., Urban Sanitary District, Rural Sanitary District, and Ecclesiastical Parish or District of*———," following this order of preference where the boundaries are conflicting. Make the next entry on the first line of the following page.

Persons not dwelling in HOUSES; *and Completion of the Enumeration Book*.

Enter under the proper Road, Lane, or other locality, any particulars you have obtained respecting persons not dwelling in houses but in Barns, Sheds, Caravans, &c.; in making up the totals at the foot of that page, however, the Barns, Sheds, &c., are not to be reckoned as Houses.

Having satisfied yourself of the correctness of your book, fill up the tables on pages iv and v, and sign the Declaration on page vi.

CONTRACTIONS TO BE USED BY THE ENUMERATOR.

ROAD, STREET, &c.—Write "*Rd.*" for Road; "*St.*" for Street; "*Pl.*" for Place; "*Sq.*" for Square; "*Ter.*" for Terrace.

NAMES.—Write the *First Christian Name* in full; *initials* or first letters of the other Christian names of a person who has more than one, may be inserted. When the same surnames occur several times in succession, write "do." for all such surnames except the *first*, which should be written in full. Where the *name* or *any particular is not known,* "n. k." should be entered in its place.

In the column "RELATION TO HEAD OF FAMILY," write "*Head*" for head of family; "*Daur.*" for daughter; "*Serv.*" for servant.

In the column "CONDITION AS TO MARRIAGE," write "*Mar.*" for married; "*Unm.*" for unmarried; "*W.*" for widow; "*Widr.*" for widower.

In the columns for AGE write the number of *years* carefully and distinctly in the proper column for "Males" or "Females," as the case may be; in the case of Children under One Year of age, as the age is expressed in months, write "*Mo.*" distinctly after the figures.

In the column for "RANK, PROFESSION, OR OCCUPATION," such contractions may be used as "*ag. lab.*" for agricultural labourer, but care must be taken that the contractions used are such as will be readily understood.

---

14. Sample from the Registrar General's instructions to Enumerators, 1851. The official title of this document is 'Directions respecting the manner of entering the Schedules'.

Questions can then be put to the students, asking them to consider why the enumerator's book may not be totally reliable as evidence. For example:

> The enumerator may have had difficulty in distributing and collecting the schedules in a densely packed urban area. (In fact, some had to be accompanied by police.)
>
> The illiteracy of many householders may have led them to fill in their forms inaccurately.
>
> Enumerators may not have been very able or efficient. (In their reports, Registrar Generals often remarked that enumerators were 'no better than labourers' or were 'very illiterate men'.)
>
> Mistakes were made when the information on schedules was transferred to the enumerators' books. (For instance, in the return for Long Lane in Ipswich, an enumerator misplaced the schedules for two households. When he later inserted them, he wrote 'misplaced from Trinity Square'. He still got it wrong for the rate book and street directory make it clear that one of the houses was not in Trinity Square, but lower down the lane in a row of cottages!)
>
> The elderly and unlettered may have had difficulty in stating their ages accurately, or even their birthplaces.

Raising and discussing points such as these will reinforce the idea that all historical evidence is likely to be less than perfect, and that it must always be questioned and tested for its reliability and accuracy.

Street directories

In comparison with the detail and technicalities of census enumerators' books, street directories are more easily accessible and simpler to use. Long before the late 19th century, so-called commercial directories had frequently been printed for whole counties, usually by companies like Kelly and White. However, it was only from the 1870s that directories were produced exclusively for large towns, carefully divided by streets. Like any other source, their reliability and accuracy must not be taken for granted.

These street directories list heads of household, house by house, street by street, often with their occupations [15]. Sometimes they give the name of the house or shop, and the number. When one compares two or more directories, the stated numbers of houses can cause problems, and must clearly be used with caution, because they seem to have been changed quite often.

If a directory can be found which coincides with the year of a census, as with Ipswich in 1881, then valuable cross-checking can be done: the names of people in the directory may well differ from those in the census, or be spelt differently, or the order of entries may be different. These are important points for students to recognise. In many cases, directories indicate clearly which side of a street is being listed, which direction is being followed, and where junctions or side-turnings occur ('here is Hill St., New St. & Short La.'). Thus they can help us to relate households in the census to houses shown on the

Venn Mrs., 2, the Elms
Sly Jas., 1, the Elms
Baptist Chapel, T. M. Morris,
 pastor
1 Kersey Mrs.

LONG LANE
BACK HAMLET.

Fisk Ben., *Ship inn.*
2 Gardener Wm., coachman,
 Montague cottages
4 Ethrill Thos., labourer, Montague cottages
6 Booth Joseph, boiler maker,
 Montague cottages
8 Wilding Wm., labourer, Montague cottages
 here is Trinity square

Grimwade's Cottages

10 Thompson Geo., fruiterer
12 Daniels —, brickmaker
 Vacant
 Lormer H. railway labourer
18 Cobbold Geo. labourer
21 Vacant
 Dale Hy., mariner
 Mickleborough Ed. smith's
 striker
 Finch John, labourer
 here is Canham's yard
22 Manning Jas., labourer
24 Woods Thos., labourer
26 Wheeler Chas., boot and shoe
28 Horne Herbert, mariner
30 Westcott Ben., mariner
32 Cable H., labourer
34 Cable Rd. lamplighter
36 Frankland John, labourer
38 Rowley Wm.
40 Hewett Geo. shoe riveter
42 Bartlett Joseph, labourer
44 Wells Alfred, butcher
46 Dersley G. general shop
48 Worler Thos. boot & shoemaker
50 Webb Wm. carpenter
here is Hill st. New st. & Short la.
49 Roberts Wm.
47 Giles Mrs
44 Banyard Chas. general dealer
81 Taylor Geo. labourer
82 Halls Geo. labourer

23 Bugg Jas.
31 Carman Ed. Wm. greengrocer
 here is Baker street
29 Thurston Geo. general shop
 Wasp Rd. marine store dealer
 here is Chapel yard
27 Osborn Nathan, labourer
25 Broomfield John, labourer

LOWER BARCLAY STREET
See Barclay Street, Lower

LOWER BROOK STREET
See Brook Street, Lower

LOWER KING STREET
ELM ST. AND ARCADE ST.

Fisher Chas. beer retailer
17 Dixey Daniel, fish merchant, &c
15 Holden Mrs. S. greengrocer
11 & 13 Saul Mrs. F. *Swan Hotel,*
 family and commercial
9 Stearn & Sons, painters, plum-
 bers, house decorators, &c
 here is the New Corn Exchange
 aad Corn Hill

LOWER ORWELL STREET
See Orwell street Lower

LYONS COURT
ELM STREET.

Spear Phlp., boot & shoemaker
King Mrs. stay maker
Cooper Mrs. nurse
Jewell Geo. tailor
Hazell Stephen, horse clipper
Lambert Aron, ostler
Last Thos. bricklayer
Bennett Henry, wheelwright &
 carriage maker
Smith Hy. labourer
Croft Mrs. B. charwoman
Sayer Robt. boot & shoemaker

MAJOR'S CORNER
CARR STREET.

70 & 72 Churchyard G., dining and
 refreshment rooms
74 Upson & Mason, butchers and
 cattle dealers
 here is Upper Orwell street

15. Extract from *Steven's Directory of Ipswich and Neighbourhood* (1881), p. 142, relating to Long Lane.

NAME OF OCCUPIER.	NAME OF OWNER.	Description of Property Rated.	Name or Situation of Property.	Estimated Extent.	Gross Estimated Rental.	Rateable Value.
				a. r. p.	£ s. d.	£ s. d.

Carr Street

NAME OF OCCUPIER.	NAME OF OWNER.	Description of Property Rated.	Name or Situation of Property.	Estimated Extent.	Gross Estimated Rental.	Rateable Value.
Carrington Ralph	M. Upson	House & Yard		14 5	12 10	
Walter Beecroft	do	Barhouse & Yard		26	22	
Frederick Fish	F. Fish	House Buildings Stables & Yard		100	90	
Frederick Barker	S. P. Clossen	House & Garden		40	34	
William Eades	N. Cattermole	House Buildings & Garden		30	26	
Samuel Barber	S. L. Clements	House Bate Office & Yard		26	23	
Frederick Greatrex	S. Pells	House & Yard		10 10	9 5	
— Johnson	do	House & Yard		10	8 10	
Frederick Geo Grangrass	do	House & Yard		12	10 10	
William Withers	do	House & Yard		10 10	9	
Robert Knights	M & R Steven	House Shop Buildings & Yard		22	19	
Henry W. Steven for tenements occupied by	do	Shop		7 5	6	
Webb	do	House & Shop		12	10 10	
William Beverley	Co operative Stores Comp	House Shop Bate Office & Buildings		90	81	
Thomas Budley Smith	N. P. Barker	House & Shop		15	13	
John Sibbenham	S. Kindred	House Shop & Yard		20	17	
Herbert Inwood Harrison	Haggar	House & Garden		30	26	
Frederick Morse	L. Morse	House Coachhouse Stables Garden 2 Cottages & Buildings		} 135	121 10	
Charles Cullingham	C. Cullingham	Stable & Yard		8	7	
Thomas Newton	S. C. Cobbold	Building		3 17	3 5	
George Scheuerman	do	Building		3 17	3 5	
William Foss		House & Yard		12	10 10	
Hancock	S. C. Cobbold	Building		3	2 10	
B. S. Carrington	do	Building		2	1 12 6	
John Orton	do	Building		3 10	2 17 6	
Elizabeth Heston	do	Cross Keys Inn Stables & Yard 2 S		20	17	
George Scheuerman	Barns	House Shop & Yard		16	14	
Robert Cracknell	S. Morris Devisees	House Shop & Yard		20	17	
			done		709 14	617 15

16. Extract from the Poor-Rate Book of St Margaret's parish, Ipswich, May 1881, relating to part of Carr Street.

town plan, and to make possible a detailed reconstruction of a street or a community (a task which cannot be done from the census alone). Sometimes directories add information which is not given in the census. For example, at Ipswich, George Thompson of Long Lane in the Rope Walk area was described in the census as a 'visitor' in the household of Mary Sargent, a widow, but the directory gives him as 'householder' and his occupation as 'fruiterer'. Similarly, William Daniels is a 'labourer' in the census, but a 'brickmaker' in the directory.

Poor-rate books

The fourth of the key sources is the borough poor-rate book. For the parishes of Ipswich such books survive from the early 1850s, but their survival elsewhere is very variable. They replace the overseers' rate books of the period prior to 1834, when the Poor Law Amendment Act introduced printed books to formalise what had been a very haphazard system of assessment. They list, street by street, the occupiers of all properties, their owners, the gross estimated rental and the rateable value [16]. Each property is briefly described ('house and shop', 'house and yard', 'house, stable and chaisehouse', etc.), sometimes with the house number in the street or its name.

Rate books, if available, can be of particular use in the study of a street or neighbourhood because:

They allow for the study of *owners*, and not just occupiers.
The value of a property can often help to establish its *boundaries* on the town plan.
They give some, if bare, information about the *sites* of individual properties.

II

ORGANISING THE WORK: INITIAL DECISIONS

Assuming that by this stage the area for study has been chosen, the site or sites visited, the key sources introduced and some work done on the historical background, it is now necessary to consider the best way of organising the classwork and assigning tasks. Starting with the census, what size should the sample be? How large the chosen area? How much time will students have for exploring the material, and producing their course-work? Clearly it is important to have enough information to get meaningful results, but not too much; otherwise the task will be overwhelming. The suggestions that follow may well have to be modified in the light of your own teaching situation. Several factors are involved, for instance the size of the group and, not least, the funds available for providing the necessary xeroxes and other resources!

The two examples used here, for the Rope Walk area and Carr Street in Ipswich, each involved approximately seventy households. This meant providing a total of 25 pages from enumerators' books, and some 20 sheets drawn from directories and rate books. Useful work can certainly be achieved on this small scale, if the analysis is done carefully and accurately, but nevertheless some teachers might prefer to have more to work on — perhaps up to double the amount of copying.

Assuming the class to number about thirty, it might be best to work in groups of four or five, each group having its own pack of documents. The first stage must be to transcribe onto specially prepared cards the details for each household as recorded in the enumerator's book. This can probably be done in two double lessons, with each group transcribing about thirty households (assuming that the total number of households will be about twice the size of the Ipswich examples, about two hundred and fifty). The teacher will have to allot a set number of households to each group, by reference to the schedule numbers in the left-hand column of the enumerator's book, thus:

> Group 1 — schedule numbers 1-28
> Group 2 — schedule numbers 29-57
> [and so on]

Cards are suggested for this work because they will stand up to heavy use better than sheets of paper. They should be prepared before work starts, and laid out as shown [17].

For the sake of clarity, students should use CAPITAL LETTERS when transcribing. They ought not to find the work laborious or boring, especially if the good reasons for doing it are fully explained to them:

17

1881 SCHEDULE NO. 82	ADDRESS LONG LANE, ST HELENS No.30 THE CAUSEWAY				NAME OF HEAD WESTCOTT, Benjamin OCCUPATION SEAMAN	
BENJAMIN WESTCOTT	HEAD	MARRIED	45		SEAMAN	MIDDX. MARYLEBONE
SOPHIA WESTCOTT	WIFE	MARRIED		45		KENT
BENJAMIN WESTCOTT	SON	UNMARR.	18		COREMAKER AT FACTORY	ESSEX. HARWICH
THOMAS WESTCOTT	SON	UNMARR.	17		BOILERMAKER	'' HARWICH
EMMA WESTCOTT	DAUGHTER	UNMARR.		13	SCHOLAR	'' HARWICH
JOHN WESTCOTT	SON	UNMARR.	10		SCHOLAR	SUFFOLK. IPSWICH
SOPHIA WESTCOTT	DAUGHTER	UNMARR.		5	SCHOLAR	'' IPSWICH
WILLIAM WESTCOTT	SON	UNMARR.	3			'' IPSWICH

17. Index card for recording each household in census returns: a suggested layout.

1) It puts the information into a more readily accessible and clear form, as a preliminary to analysis.
2) It will familiarise them with the content and layout of the original.
3) It will, we hope, arouse their interest in the personal details of individual households, relationships and occupations.

Incidentally, it is important to make out a card for any uninhabited houses, and to file the information in the same order as it occurs in the enumerator's book.

For teachers, the resulting bank of information becomes a permanent resource for use by other classes, and can be extended when money is found to buy more photocopies. Indeed, the potential is considerable for expanding this work into a major project for young historians throughout the school. Where the data can be stored on computer disks, it can be used not only in history classes, but in integrated studies which involve, for example, mathematics and statistics. Of course, the computerised use of census returns is not unknown in schools, but that raises other and wider issues than those being explored here.

III

STUDY AREA 1: A WORKING-CLASS DISTRICT

The essential purpose of work on the key sources is to try to re-create the social and physical environment in which past generations lived. The focus is on individuals, their families and households, and on the general structure of the local community. The aim is to understand better the lives of people in the past, and to make fruitful comparisons, where possible, between the past and the present.

When working on a street or residential area, students should be encouraged to ask essential questions such as these:

What were the sizes of households in the street?
What was the average size?
How does this compare with the present day?
What questions are raised by the comparison, and what conclusions can be drawn from it?

What was the age-structure of the inhabitants?
How does this compare with the present day?
What questions are raised by the comparison, and what light does it throw on the social life of a late Victorian community?

How does the information about birthplaces tell us about migration? What kinds of migration are involved?
Does the evidence of the census help us to understand why people moved?

What kinds of work was the population of the street engaged in?
What was the precise nature of each trade and occupation?

Further questions will arise when the census is related to other sources:

What light is thrown on housing and living conditions?
How does the evidence help us to re-create the environment in which people lived?
How far does the evidence allow us to 're-populate' the street?

These questions, which demand an analysis of the evidence before we can generalise and draw conclusions, will only be effectively explored if we persuade our students to use sound methods in their work. The ways that are suggested in the following examples are neither unique nor other than straightforward and practical, but should provide sufficient guidance.

19

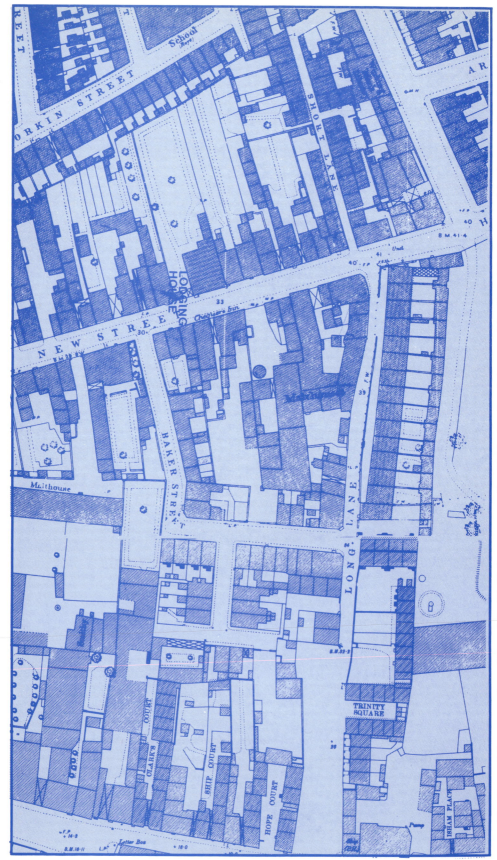

18. **Part of the town plan of Ipswich, 10.56 feet to one mile, 1881**, showing that part of the Rope Walk area used in the examples of analysis (pp. 19-36).

Household size

A total of 71 households lived in our sample area in the Rope Walk district of Ipswich. They resided in three courts (Clark's Court, Ship Court and Hope Court), in the cottages on the east side of Long Lane and in cottages in Short Lane [18]. The following table shows how households can be analysed and the results clearly tabulated:

| | Number of people in each household | | | | | | | | | | | | |
---	1	2	3	4	5	6	7	8	9	10	11	12	Total
Number of households	0	15	15	8	12	6	5	6	2	0	1	1	71
Total of population per size of household	0	30	45	32	60	36	35	48	18	0	11	12	327

$$\text{Thus, average (mean) household size} = \frac{\text{total population}}{\text{no. of households}} = \frac{327}{71} = 4.6$$

To explain the significance of such a straightforward analysis, a comparison could be made between this sample of the population in 1881 and the average household size today. The returns of *The Office of Population Census and Surveys: Key Statistics for Local Authorities* (published by HMSO in 1984 on the basis of the 1981 census) should be obtainable in local public libraries. For example, in 1981 the average household in Ipswich had only 2.67 persons. Other important questions then arise: what accounts for this difference in the size of households? Why did only 3.4 per cent of Ipswich's population in 1981 live in households of more than five persons, whereas in 1881 as many as 47 per cent lived in such households? Furthermore, is it valid to compare a few streets in 1881 with the whole town in 1981?

Age structure

An analysis of age-structure is best done by extracting the information by sex, and in five-year periods [19], and then translating the results into a bar-chart. This could be done by getting each group to work on their own schedules, using a simple form for the purpose, and then aggregating all the results. The resulting 'pyramid' [20] should raise questions, especially about the large numbers of young people (under 15) and the small sizes of the older age-groups. These characteristics are most obvious when, again, comparisons are made with today, thus:

Age-group	Rope Walk, 1881	Ipswich, 1981
0-14	45%	22.4%
15-24	15%	14.2%
25-44	26%	25.2%
45+	14%	38.2%

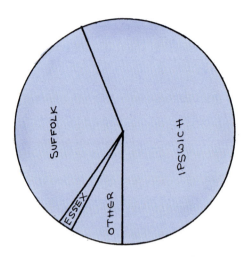

AGE GROUP	0-4	5-9	10-14	15-19	20-24	25-29	30-34	35-39	40-44	45-49	50-54	55-59	60-64	65-69	70-
MALES															
TOTAL	19	11	11	15	10	6	5	6	5	5	5	1	5	3	1
FEMALES															
TOTAL	19	18	12	11	9	9	6	7	3	8	4	2	4	3	0

19. **Age structure**: a simple form for tabulating ages in five-year groups.

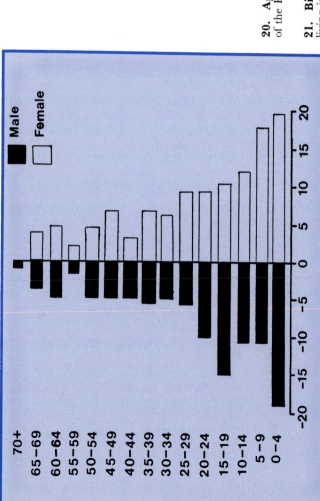

20. **Age structure expressed as a bar chart**: the population of the Rope Walk area, 1881.

21. **Birthplaces shown by pie chart**: the birthplaces of those living in the Rope Walk area, 1881.

In this way, the significance of the pattern in 1881 is highlighted, and we can appreciate more clearly how different was the social world of a hundred years ago.

After carrying out an analysis of Victorian households and ages, a class could then focus on various aspects of social life where dramatic changes have occurred since the 1880s, such as the use of family planning, improved standards of health, higher life expectancy and better housing. This might also be an opportunity for discussing some of the undoubted defects of modern society!

Birthplaces

This work might profitably start with the birthplaces of heads of household. Results can be tabulated as follows:

	Percentage
Born in Ipswich	56.3
Born elsewhere in Suffolk	33.8
Born in Essex	1.5
Born in other English counties	8.4
Born outside England	0.0

The county of Essex was included separately because Ipswich lies quite close to the county boundary. The same analysis could then be expressed diagramatically as a pie-diagram [21].

From this, more detailed kinds of analysis might follow. For example, the birthplaces of residents in the Rope Walk area suggest that many people migrated over fairly short distances from parishes surrounding Ipswich. This information could easily be mapped, with numbers or arrows of varying thickness to show the strength of migration from different sources, and questions will arise as to the causes of this movement. Examples of migration over longer distances will also be found. Witness, for example, the list of those staying in a lodging-house in New Street [23]. Analysis shows that two-thirds of the lodgers had been born as far away as Yorkshire, Northumberland, Leicestershire, London, Kent and even Ireland. A large percentage of the lodgers were male; 45 per cent were young men, and 72 per cent were unmarried. Such evidence of migrant labour, of men 'on the tramp', and of the role of the common lodging-house, could be related to larger historical questions about 19th-century migration and be explored against other sources, primary and secondary, general and local [22, 24, 25]. Again, comparisons with the labour market in the 1980s might prove stimulating to discussion. So, small but illuminating examples from sources like the census can have great potential for the study of major themes.

The birthplaces of children, as recorded in the census, provide another important method of analysis, for they can reveal how recently a family had moved in and how migratory it had been in recent years. For instance, if it is asked which of these three households is likely to have come to Ipswich most recently, the point is made:

Name	Age	Birthplace
Henry Mayhew	26	Tunstall, Suffolk
Alice Mayhew	21	Playford, Suffolk
Alice Mayhew	2	Colva[?] Green, Suffolk
George Mayhew	6 mo.	Lt Bealings, Suffolk
Joseph Booth	30	Lincoln
Eliza Booth	29	Derby
Alice Booth	9	Lincoln
Anne Booth	3	Lincoln
Philip Draycott	25	Spalding, Lincs.
Emma Draycott	28	Holbeach, Lincs.
Gertrude Draycott	4 mo.	Holbeach, Lincs.

Students should be reminded that migration can only be studied in this way for those households which contained children. In addition, the evidence does not tell us when precisely any migrants arrived. Therefore, students must be warned that, when they write up their results, their statements, inferences and conclusions will have to be very carefully weighed, and will be less assertive and certain than they might hope. For example, 'It is probable that the Mayhew family came to Ipswich within the six months prior to the taking of the census', and not 'They did arrive . . .'.

So one Friday in the summer of 1845 I left my old master for good and ever, and having arranged my little affairs, left home on the Monday following, for Lancashire. I walked to Hebden Bridge and took a train for Rochdale, my first railway ride . . . .

Sleeping at Rochdale I walked forward to Oldham, got work, started at dinner-time, and worked a half-day on the Tuesday after leaving home. After securing lodgings at night, I wrote home in a very hopeful strain. My wages at first were 28s. per week, increased afterwards at time and time to 32s. . . .

I started work at Hibberts, Platts, now Platts Brothers, Oldham, one of the largest machine-shops in England . . .

After working here thirteen or fourteen months, I, along with fifty others, got stopped. I was told to come again in a few weeks and see if anything turned up. This was on the Saturday. On Tuesday following I left Oldham and walked to Huddersfield. The day after I walked to Leeds, and for the second time in my life slept in a common lodging house. Such abomination was a disgrace to the town, and the century. They are all under supervision now, and not before the need was felt.

The day following I walked to York. The day was wet, but after looking into lots of public houses without finding a fire walked the streets till near bedtime. I then obtained a share of a bed for 1s. but got my jacket and waistcoat dried. I took the train next morning at 5.45 for Darlington, and about 9 o'clock breakfasted on nearly black bread with a crust like a board and some skimmed milk cost 2d. . . .

I started here at 23s. per week. It was a small engine-shop with no proper order or economical way of working . . .

23. Extract from the autobiography of Thomas Wood, Engineer: a vivid example from the 1840s of a migrant worker in the north of England, taken from J. Burnett, *Useful Toil* (1974), pp. 309-11.

Road, street	Name	Relation to Head	Condition	Age M	Age F	Occupation	Where Born
28 New Street	Adin Barnes	Head	M	38		Lodging House Keeper	Cambs: Soham
	Alice ,,	Wife	M		38		Suff: Stowmarket
	Adin T. ,,	Son	U	16			Ipswich
	Emma ,,	Dau.	U		14		London W.
	William ,,	Son	U	13			Ipswich
	Samuel ,,	Son	U	11			Cambs: Soham
	Edward ,,	Son	U	9			London
	Henry Hines	Lodger	U	22		Drover	Ipswich
	Robert Dale	Lodger	U	26		Tailor	York
	Philip Draycott	Head	M	25		Tailor	Lincs: Spalding
	Emma ,,	Wife	M		28		Lincs: Holbeach
	Gertrude ,,	Dau.	U		4m		Lincs: ,,
	John Gray	Lodger	U	42		Boiler Maker	Lincoln
	William Burrows	Lodger	U	35		Bricklayer	Yorks: Leeds
	John Drount	Lodger	U	17		Labourer	Essex: Maldon
	George Syrett	Lodger	U	20		Seaman	Suff: Bildeston
	Charles Alger	Lodger	U	21		Labourer	Kent: Bromley
	William Farthing	Lodger	U	62		Butcher	Ipswich
	Thomas Stokes	Head	M	48		Gardener	Kent: Bearsted
	Eliza ,,	Wife	M		27		Kent: Gt Gidding
	George Fletcher	Head	M	29		Bricklayer	Ipswich
	Ann ,,	Wife	M		25		,,
	Ambrose Draper	Head	M	27		Hawker	Suff: Brandeston
	Annie ,,	Wife	M		27	Hawker	Suff: ,,
	? ,,	Dau.	U		6m		Suff: ,,
	David Izzard	Lodger	U	32		Bricklayer	Surrey: Lambeth
	William Dale	Head	M	25		Stonemason	York
	Fanny ,,	Wife	M		24		Southampton
	John Mead	Lodger	Widr	35		Smith	Leicester
	James Stone	Lodger	U	35		Tailor	London: St George-in-the-East
	William Baxter	Lodger	U	40		Hawker	Suff: Woodbridge
	William Johnson	Lodger	U	42		Bricklayer	Essex: Braintree
	John Jones	Lodger	U	24		Labourer	Kent: Dover
	William C. Sibley	Lodger	U	21		Seaman	Beds
	Ralph Waite	Head	M	45		Iron Moulder	Berwick-on-Tweed
	Mary ,,	Wife	M		38		Hants: Lymington
	Edward Murrell	Lodger	U	34		Licensed Hawker	Inniskillen

22. Extract from an enumerator's book, 1881: giving the inhabitants of a lodging-house in New Street, Ipswich. Apart from the keeper and his family, all those listed are lodgers (M = married; U = unmarried). This was one of three lodging-houses in that street in 1881.

A variety of poor people were constantly shifting in and out of the main centres of population, some leaving the towns to make long, slow foot-journeys through the country-side.

In sharp contrast to the settled inhabitants of the countryside, these nomads were the least charted section of contemporary society. Many familiar wayside types remained more mysterious than the occupants of the darkest urban warren. About the only certain characteristic of this floating, heterogeneous population was that it was never constant. Not only was it to a great extent seasonal, but its numbers and composition were affected by the state of trade, the incidence of public works, the tides of immigration, the activities of police and poor law officials, and a whole host of agencies, local and national.

One important, ever-fluctuating class of wanderers consisted of men in search of some particular type of work. The end of a large job might release hundreds of navvies: in a district of big arable farms the harvest would attract scores of migrant field workers. At such times large gangs of labourers, which might include some women and children, would drift through an area, coalescing and dispersing as they went. When a regional industry suffered prolonged depression, considerable parties might be set off on the trek together, drawn by reports of a demand for labour somewhere else.

Less conspicuous, and less troublesome to residents in the neighbourhoods through which they passed, were the men who moved around on their own or with one or two occasional companions, trying their luck at place after place. At times there were numbers of trained artisans roving about in this fashion, journeymen who visited their trade's particular 'house of call' in each town in turn in hopes of discovering an opening.

Going off on the tramp was a recognised means of avoiding a local slump at home and improving one's prospects, even in better paid crafts.

24. Extract from K. Chesney, *The Victorian Underworld* (1971), pp. 60-1. Note the causes which the author gives for labourers moving in search of work. For a fascinating study of this, see 'Comers and Goers', by R. Samuel, in *The Victorian City*, edited by H. Dyos and M. Woolf (1973).

Nevertheless, by using such information alongside another of the key sources, the rate book, the subject of mobility can be probed from another direction. For instance, rate books were compiled in the May and November of each year; the census of 1881 was taken on 3 April. By comparing a list of occupiers in the rate book of November 1880 with those in the census, we find that, of 24 names listed for Long Lane in the first source, only 15 appear in the second. A simple exercise like this therefore reveals that a considerable proportion of households had moved within a period of six months. Similar, if inevitably cruder, comparisons can be made by examining successive censuses, at ten-year intervals, but where sources like rate books survive we should try to get a more precise focus on the problem — especially for working-class areas.

These four different ways of analysing the data on birthplaces demonstrate that specific aspects of working-class communities can be satisfactorily investigated, and that the evidence can be marshalled and organised to produce quite a sophisticated historical analysis — providing students are prepared to weigh the evidence carefully.

Five of those moral and physical pests of a town, *common lodging houses*, exist in Ipswich: three in St. Clement's, and two in St. Margaret's. One is a licensed victualler's house, one a beer house, and the other three are private houses. Four out of the five have large sleeping rooms, filled with stump bedsteads made of wood, having on them flock or straw beds. Upon these the vagrants of both sexes and of all ages sleep. Each bed is furnished with a pair of sheets, a blanket, and a rug, which are frequently in the most filthy condition. Ventilation of the rooms is entirely out of the question. The parish authorities, during the last year, compelled the proprietors of some of these houses to whitewash and otherwise clean the sleeping apartments. Each lodger is charged three-pence per night, and, before retiring to rest, must pay or be turned into the street. In most of the rooms there are eight or nine bedsteads; frequently three persons sleep in a bed, and married and single in the same room. No one is required to wash before going to bed, except those who may have been walking on a wet day, without shoes or stockings, whose feet have in that case to undergo the process of ablution. These houses are the receptacles for beggars, thieves, and prostitutes, as well as for some poor creatures whose miserable existence compels them to lodge at the lowest possible cost. The police regard them as places where the dangerous classes are to be found; and, during our fairs or races, they are so full that the pickpocket and the homeless wanderer, the poor artizan's wife and the prostitute, the innocent child and the young of both sexes just ripening into felons, may there be seen crowded together: English, Irish, Scotch, Welsh, and Hanoverians may be said to be completely packed in these places at such times. The positive viciousness, filthy habits, and utter contempt of decency there seen, is in the highest degree disgusting; and the babel that arises from the confused and violent conversation of the occupants, is a sad chorus to the Christian's ear. A peep into one of these places on a Sunday morning would greatly surprise many of our inhabitants. Some of the lodgers are cooking, some card playing, some cleaning their clothes, and others remaining in bed, whilst confusion and noise every-where prevail.

These places are bad in all respects; but where else can the poor creatures go? Decent lodgings in the town they cannot pay for. The establishment of a model lodging house is the only remedy for this evil; and even in a commercial point of view, the erection of one would be a good speculation. The enormous profits the proprietors of the present deplorable lodging houses are reaping, show it to be quite certain that a high rate of interest would be obtained from the capital invested; whilst a material diminution of vice and misery would not less certainly be secured. In one of these houses, we are told that the proprietor considers fifty lodgers per night a very small number, and he has received as many as 120 in one night.

25. **Extract from John Glyde**, *The Moral, Social and Religious Condition of Ipswich* (1850), pp. 58-60, describing lodging-houses in Ipswich.

Occupations

As students comb the census returns, they will no doubt find many trades and occupations which are obscure or unknown to them, and they should be encouraged to find out what was involved. Much useful work can be done with dictionaries, especially if the school library contains *The Shorter Oxford Dictionary* or its equivalent. For example, the census for Ipswich listed, among many others, the following occupations which would probably cause mystification for most young people today:

Cooper	Core Maker
Marine Store Dealer	Boiler Maker
Hawker	Staymaker
Whitesmith	Annuitant
Drover	Currier
Cordwainer	Compositor
Engine Turner	Muffin Maker
Iron Moulder	Mason

The nature of certain trades can be explored more deeply. Teachers may, for instance, be able to take advantage of surviving examples of particular industries, crafts or trades in their own areas, or they may have a good local museum to call on. For some less familiar trades, contemporary descriptions may help. Take, for example, what Charles Dickens wrote about a 'marine store' [26].

The reader must often have perceived in some by-street, in a poor neighbourhood, a small dirty shop, exposing for sale the most extraordinary and confused jumble of old, worn-out, wretched articles, that can well be imagined. Our wonder at their ever having been bought, is only equalled by our astonishment at the idea of their ever being sold again. On a board, at the side of the door, are placed about twenty books — all odd volumes; and as many wine-glasses — all different patterns; several locks, an old earthenware pan, full of rusty keys; two or three gaudy chimney ornaments — cracked, of course; the remains of a lustre, without any drops; a round frame like a capital O, which has once held a mirror; a flute, complete with the exception of the middle joint; a pair of curling-irons; and a tinder-box. In front of the shop-window, are ranged some half-dozen high-backed chairs, with spinal complaints and wasted legs; a corner cupboard; two or three very dark mahogany tables with flaps like mathematical problems; some pickle-bottles, some surgeons' ditto, with gilt labels and without stoppers; an unframed portrait of some lady who flourished about the beginning of the thirteenth century, by an artist who never flourished at all; an incalculable host of miscellanies of every description, including armour and cabinets, rags and bones, fenders and street-door knockers, fire-irons, wearing apparel and bedding, a hall-lamp, and a room-door. Imagine, in addition to this incongruous mass, a black doll in a white frock, with two faces — one looking up the street, and the other looking down, swinging over the door; a board with the squeezed-up inscription "Dealer in marine stores," in lanky white letters, whose height is strangely out of proportion to their width; and you have before you precisely the kind of shop to which we wish to direct your attention.

26. Extract from Henry Mayhew, *London Labour and the London Poor*, taken from P. Quennell (ed.), *Mayhew's London* (1969), pp. 204-5.

Before students start working on local occupations, they might benefit from a classroom exercise using a list of occupations and general and specialist dictionaries to investigate the precise nature of each, and finally putting them into appropriate general categories. It could be based on this random sample taken from census abstracts covering the whole country:

Actuary	Lighterman
Animal Dealer	Lithographer
Awl Maker	Mercer
Bleeder	Oilcake Dealer
Brazier	Orris Weaver
Broker	Parish Clerk
Calico Dyer	Pilot
Carrier	Poulterer
Chelsea Pensioner	Proprietor of Houses
Doffer Plate Maker	Sawyer
Fellmonger	Seamstress
Fuller	Stevedore
Gimlet Maker	Straw Plait Dealer
Gutta Percha Dealer	Surveyor
Huckster	Tallow Chandler
Joiner Knacker	Tanner
Knacker	Tinker

It might also be worth pointing out that some of these occupations have given rise to long-standing surnames. Why not all of them? Then, the information needs to be grouped or categorised under different general classes of trades and occupations. This presents difficulties which students will soon recognise, particularly where categories overlap. A full list of occupational categories can be found in census abstracts, but at this level simplified groupings can prove effective, thus:

Agriculture (arable and pastoral)
Mining, Quarrying
Manufactures (machinery and tools, shipbuilding, metals, textiles, etc.)
Commerce (merchants, bankers, etc.)
Building
Transport (by road, rail and water)
Dealing (raw materials, clothing, food and drink, etc.)
Public Services (central and local government, police, etc.)
The Professions (law, medicine, education, religion, etc.)
Property Owners, and those with Independent Means
Domestic Service (maids, cooks, chars, grooms, etc.)
Labourers

The work done by its inhabitants is fundamental to our understanding of any historical community. First, the occupations should be listed and totalled. This is best done by sex (male and female separately) and by age-group. Some occupations listed in the census should be excluded because they are not genuine examples of gainful employment, for example 'scholar' and 'wife of sailor'. It should, however, be noted that some wives were undoubtedly assisting their husbands in their work, such as 'farmer's wife', so they deserve inclusion. Those people listed without occupations must also be noted.

Work on the Rope Walk area, though based on a small sample from the enumerators' books, nonetheless clearly confirms the working-class nature of the community. Some 46 per cent of the employed males were manual labourers or unskilled workers (such as coal porters and lamplighters), 12 per cent had occupations connected with ships, the port and the sea (sailors, mariners, a shipwright), 10 per cent were in the

Table 10 *continued.*—OCCUPATIONS of MALES and FEMALES in the EASTERN DIVISION and its REGISTRATION COUNTIES, and in each URBAN SANITARY DISTRICT of which the POPULATION exceeds 50,000 PERSONS.

OCCUPATIONS.	URBAN SANITARY DISTRICTS.					
	WEST HAM.		IPSWICH.		NORWICH.	
	Males.	Females.	Males.	Females.	Males.	Females.
3. *Cotton and Flax*						
Cotton, Cotton goods, Manufacture	34	150	1	1	4	121
Cotton, Calico—Printer, Dyer, Bleacher	3	.	.	.	.	.
Cotton, Calico—Warehouseman, Dealer	1	.	.	.	.	.
Flax, Linen—Manufacturer, Dealer	3	1	.	.	.	.
Lace Manufacturer, Dealer	1	13	1	2	2	3
Fustian Manufacturer, Dealer	.	.	.	.	.	.
Tape Manufacturer, Dealer	.	.	.	.	.	.
Thread Manufacturer, Dealer	.	.	.	.	.	.
4. *Hemp and other Fibrous Materials.*						
Hemp, Jute, Cocoa Fibre, Manufacture	98	374	.	.	6	.
Rope, Twine, Cord—Maker, Dealer	15	2	8	.	40	.
Mat Maker, Seller	31	13	6	2	9	7
Net Maker	1	.	.	.	1	3
Canvas, Sailcloth, Manufacture	.	2	.	.	.	.
Sacking, Sack, Bag—Maker, Dealer	9	87	7	25	4	6
Others working and dealing in Hemp	.	.	.	.	2	1
5. *Mixed or Unspecified Materials.*						
Weaver (undefined)	6	24	.	.	65	142
Dyer, Printer, Scourer, Bleacher, Calenderer (undefined)	10	8	9	6	64	16
Factory hand (Textile, undefined)	3	4	.	.	9	202
Felt Manufacture	1	.	.	.	.	.
Carpet, Rug, Manufacture	7	.	.	.	3	.
Manchester Warehouseman	5	.	.	.	5	.
Draper, Linen Draper, Mercer	218	183	158	114	52	294
Fancy Goods (Textile), Manufacturer, Worker, Dealer	7	27	.	6	6	65
Trimming Maker, Dealer	7	19	.	.	1	8
Embroiderer	1	16	.	4	1	1
Others	.	1	.	.	.	.
18. PERSONS WORKING AND DEALING IN DRESS.						
1. *Dress.*						
Hatter, Hat Manufacture (not straw)	31	5	13	1	21	4
Straw—Hat, Bonnet, Plait, Manufacture	3	8	.	11	.	11
Tailor	247	167	327	512	562	894
Milliner, Dressmaker, Staymaker	15	1429	34	1659	.	1909
Shawl Manufacture	.	.	.	.	1	5
Shirt Maker, Seamstress	15	554	.	231	2	254
Hosiery Manufacture	.	1	.	.	1	.
Hosier, Haberdasher	38	16	9	3	14	8
Glover, Glove Maker	3	8	5	13	7	20
Button Maker, Dealer	1	3	.	.	.	.
Shoe, Boot—Maker, Dealer	480	41	785	185	3286	1772
Patten, Clog, Maker	6	.	.	.	11	.
Wig Maker, Hairdresser	91	1	35	4	41	1
Umbrella, Parasol, Stick—Maker, Dealer	18	10	3	4	11	5
Accoutrement Maker	.	.	.	.	.	.
Old Clothes Dealer, and others	5	9	2	10	5	17

27.   Sample of a census abstract or printed report from the *Census of England and Wales, 1881, Division IV (Eastern Counties)*, p. 153, Table 10: Occupations of Males and Females.

Another experience I had some nine years after the previous. I was pregnant, work had been very scarce, and I was in a very weak state. My husband had been at work three weeks when he happened an accident. He had fallen from a high scaffold. The Clerk of the Works came to tell me they had taken him to the hospital, and I had better go at once and take someone with me. Of course, I thought the worst had happened. (He did not know my condition.) I was between three and four months, and this shock caused a miscarriage. I had a midwife, who, no doubt, was all right when things were straightforward. I got about again, but was very weak and ill. He was in hospital six weeks. I took in needlework. I got very weak yet very stout. I thought it was through sitting so much at the machine. I worked and starved myself to make sick pay, 12s. per week, go as far as possible. I got so weak, and fainted several times after heavy days at the machine. I was taken very ill one night, and my daughter went for the doctor. He said: "We must have her in bed," and sent for a neighbour. It was a confinement of a seven-months babe. When he told me it was childbirth, I said it was impossible, for I had miscarried about four months previous. However, it was true. I had been carrying twins — a most peculiar case — during that four months. My system was being drained, and the worry and anxiety had effect on the child. It was weak and did not move much. I had a bad time, but the child lived for nine months, but a very delicate child.

———————————

I was married in 1887. My husband had just left the Army; he got work as a porter in a bedding warehouse. This firm failed, and he and the book-keeper joined forces and began in the bedding trade in a small way, and we were married. I went every day except Saturday to the shop to cut out and sew. My husband's wages were £1 per week; we did our own housework at night, and I baked and ironed on Saturday morning. When my boy was born, twelve months after marriage, my husband's wages were 25s.; of course, I could earn nothing. In another twelve months my second baby (a girl) was born. We removed to —, where rents were cheap, and I was a stranger. I took in plain sewing and washing, and cut up my clothes for my babies. I had a good stock of clothes, I may say.

28. Extract from M. Llewellyn Davies, *Maternity: Letters from Working Women* (1915), Letters 12 and 44.

clothing trades (eight shoemakers, a cordwainer and a tailor), and another 10 per cent were in dealing (butcher, shopkeeper, errand boy and marine store dealer). From this kind of analysis students will be able to highlight the dominant forms of employment, and to understand the nature of what people actually did in their jobs. As we have already seen, our marine dealer actually dealt in second-hand 'junk', and was not doing what we might have expected of him.

The analysis of female occupations can also raise major questions of interpretation. The number of employed women may well be small, as in the Ipswich sample, but interesting patterns can be revealed by relating occupations to age-groups and to 'marital condition':

Female Occupations in the Rope Walk Area

Marital Status	Age-groups						
	13-19	20-29	30-39	40-49	50-59	60+	Total
Married, occupied	0	0	1	1	0	0	2
Married, unoccupied	0	29	19	12	6	3	69
Unmarried, occupied	11	7	1	0	0	0	18
Unmarried, unoccupied	4	1	0	0	0	0	5
Widows, occupied	0	0	2	2	1	0	5
Widows, unoccupied	0	0	0	1	0	1	2
Total of individuals	15	37	23	16	7	4	101

What questions are raised by such an analysis? The pattern shows that most young, unmarried girls and women were working, but very few married women. Why was this? Why apparently were so few teenage girls living in the area? What percentage of all females were occupied? What percentage of unmarried females over the age of 13 were occupied? And so on.

Analysis of this kind also highlights the nature of women's work. Of the 25 occupied females, 10 were servants or chars, seven were staymakers and five tailoresses: domestic service and the 'sweated' trades are clearly evident. If the abstracts of censuses are available [27], students could investigate whether the local pattern was typical of the town as a whole: in Ipswich staymaking was certainly an important source of female employment. (What, incidentally, was staymaking?) Having analysed female occupations in this way, the local pattern can then be related to the wider question of women's work in the 19th century, and the evidence which exists for it. Once again, the source can be questioned: how accurate is the census in recording women's work? Was seasonal and casual work likely to be recorded? Would the work of the two women, whose testimony is given above [28], have been entered in the census?

Housing

Given the key sources, it should be possible to develop a considerable amount of work on this topic. The town plan offers great scope for exploring the physical environment, and for measuring precisely the ground-area of houses and cottages. Students could start by trying to locate different kinds of housing on their plan:

Are the streets terraced?
Can any back-to-back housing be seen?
Do houses abut directly on the street?
Do any houses have front gardens or 'front areas'?
Which houses have access to the rear by back alleys or by 'tunnels'?
Are there any 'courts'?
Which houses have a 'back house'?
What are the dimensions of houses?

29. Part of the town plan of Ipswich, 10.56 feet to one mile, 1881, showing the layout of houses in part of the Rope Walk area.

30. Part of the town plan of Ipswich, 10.56 feet to one mile, 1881, showing cottages on the east side of Long Lane, Ipswich (parish boundary thus: . . . .).

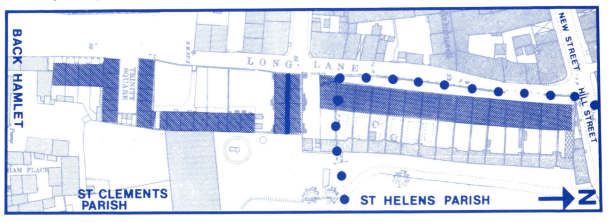

Some of the different characteristics of 19th-century housing can be seen in the accompanying map [**29**], a sample from the town plan of Ipswich depicting a small area just north of Long Lane. These streets are almost entirely made up of terraces, apart from two pairs of semi-detached houses on the north side of Arthur Street. The terraces themselves show important variations, however: the block of houses at the top left-hand side, facing Pottery Street, has bay windows and walled front 'gardens' with paths to the front door. Behind, these houses have an integral wing extending into the back yard, with toilets and sheds adjacent; the house at the south end also has a glass conservatory at the rear. With the exception of the 'semis', all the other houses on the map abut directly onto the pavement. The row of cottages at the top either lacks rear-wings or has had them added, while the toilet is at the bottom of the yard. Thus it is possible to suggest from the dimensions of the cottages and houses that they consisted 'probably' of either three rooms downstairs and two or three upstairs, or two up and two down. Only a few houses have any access to the rear for the removal of 'night soil' (excrement), refuse or, say, the delivery of coal.

Very few 'back to back' houses were built in Ipswich. These were rows of cottages whose rear wall abutted onto another row built directly behind, thus giving no yard at the back and no through-ventilation (*see*, for instance, the block of eight on the east side of Long Lane [**30**]). Many people, however, lived in 'natural' back-to-backs, in courts where houses were built against the wall of a property, on the other side of which was another row (*see* the houses without through-ventilation on the south side of Trinity Square [**30**], and the courts in Fore Street [**18**]).

Very challenging detective work can be done, using all four key sources, when students are asked to put the households mentioned in the census into the houses depicted in the town plan. This technique for re-creating a street or neighbourhood is known as 're-population'. If they are asked 'How far is this precisely possible?' and 'Which pieces of evidence help in the solution of this problem?', students will have to demonstrate how they achieved their results. Here is an example which could be used as an exercise in the classroom. It is based on:

> The town plan showing the east side of Long Lane [**30**]
> A transcript of census entries [**31**]
> A transcript of entries from the rate book for St Clement's and St Helen's
>   parishes [**32**]
> Entries from a directory [**15**]

The following are some of the points and problems that should arise. If, to start with, only the town plan and census are used, it should soon become apparent that, apart from enabling us to locate Trinity Square and the boundary between the two parishes, these two sources are of limited use on their own. When the rate book is brought into play, it can be helpful because it reveals blocks of property belonging to different owners. It is not known, however, except by guessing, whether the lists from either the census or the rate books run from north to south, or vice versa. The directory, however, gives unambiguous locations at the beginning and end of its lists which, correlated with the other sources, begin to sort out the problem of locating people in their homes.

Montague Cottages	William Garner	Coachman
Montague Cottages	Thomas Earthroll	Labourer
Montague Cottages	Daniel Wilding	Labourer
Trinity Square	Charles Orvis	Labourer
	Charles Waspe	Labourer
	Henry Mayhew	Labourer
	Henry Baalham	Labourer
	Henry Gladen	Labourer
	Jane Simpson	Milkwoman
	Henry Potter	Labourer
Grimwade's Cottages	Mary Sargent	
	William Daniels	Labourer
	Henry Lormer	Labourer
	James Gosling	Labourer
	George Cobbold	Pipemaker
	Henry Dale	Mariner
	Edward Mickleburgh	Labourer
	John Finch	Labourer
	Harry Bugg	Coal Carter
	William Plane	Shoemaker
Peck Square	Frederick Nock	Mariner
	Thomas Pizey	Labourer
	James Lambert	Coal Porter
Long Lane	Henry Gibbs	Engine Turner
Overlooked from		
Trinity Square	Richard Rice	Labourer
	Joseph Booth	Boilermaker
No. 24	Thomas Woods	Labourer
26	Robert Stederton	Tailor
28	Eliza Horne	Sailor's wife
30	Benjamen Westcott	Mariner
32	Harry Cable	Labourer
34	Richard Cable	Lamplighter
36	John Frankland	Labourer
38	Uninhabited	
40	George Hewitt	Shoemaker
42	Joseph Bartlett	Labourer
44	Alfred Wells	Butcher
46	George Dersley	Shopkeeper and Smith
48	Thomas Waller	Shoemaker
50	William Webb	Carpenter

31. Transcript of a census enumerator's book, 1881, for the east side of Long Lane, Ipswich, giving the names of heads of households, their addresses and occupations, in the order in which they were recorded.

Occupier	Owner	Description	Rateable Value
Daniel Wilding	Henry King	House No. 8	£4
Joseph Booth		House No. 6	£4
Thomas Earthroll		House No. 4	£4
William Garner		House No. 2	£4
Henry Potter	John Pells	Trinity Court House	£3
Jane Simpson		House	£3
Richard Rice		House	£3
Henry Mayhew		House	£3
Henry Baalham		House	£3
Henry Glading		House	£3
Arthur Finch		House	£3
Charles Orvis		House	£3
Serjeant	Edward Grimwade	House	£4-10-0
William Daniels		House	£3-10-0
Unoccupied		House	£3-10-0
Henry Lormer		House	£4-10-0
George Cobbold		House	£4
Unoccupied		House	£4
Henry Dale		House	£3-10-0
Edward Mickleburgh		House	£3-10-0
Alfred Dewhirst		House	£3-10-0
John Finch		House	£3-10-0
William Plane	~~N. C. Canham~~	House	£4
Thomas Pizey	Samuel Peck	House	£4
Frederick Nock		House	£4
George Lambert		House	£4
~~Hen. Gibbs~~			
James Mannell		House & Shop	£6-05-0
William Webb	T. Girling	House & Yard	£5-17-6
Henry Waller		House & Yard	£5-17-6
~~Thomas Garner~~			
Geo Dersley		House & Yard	£5-17-6
Alfred Wells		House & Yard	£5-17-6
John Bartlett		House & Yard	£5-17-6
John Hewitt		House & Yard	£5-17-6
~~John Podd~~			
Wm Rowley		House & Yard	£5-17-6
John Franklin	Mrs King	House & Yard	£5-17-6
Richard Cable		House & Yard	£5-17-6
Henry Cable		House & Yard	£5-17-6
Benjamin Westcott		House & Yard	£5-17-6
~~Elijah Sheldrake~~			
Herbert Horn		House & Yard	£5-17-6
~~Lovings Biggins~~			
Chas Wheeler		House & Yard	£5-17-6
Thomas Woods		House & Yard	£5-17-6

32. Transcript of a rate book, 1881, for the east side of Long Lane, in the parishes of St Clement's and St Helen's, Ipswich, giving names of occupiers and owners, a description of each property and its rateable value. Some names have been deleted and others substituted.

In fact, it becomes possible to re-populate 'Montague Cottages' (Nos. 2, 4 and 8) at the south end of Long Lane, and the two blocks of cottages owned by 'T. Girling' and 'Mrs. King' (Nos. 50-24). Beyond that, however, students will have to be very tentative in their conclusions. They cannot do more than generalise about Trinity Square; they should be able to locate 'Peck Square' as consisting of the single larger house referred to as 'No. 22' in the directory and as 'House and Shop' in the rate book, and the four houses that lie at right angles to the Lane; by elimination, they can say that 'Grimwade's Cottages' must comprise the four that back onto Peck Square (thus making eight back-to-back houses) and six more between there and Trinity Square.

In this example, the evidence is in many instances questionable and confusing, and more determined students would do well to come up with the following: the enumerator mistakenly put Joseph Booth as resident in Trinity Square, whereas the rate book and directory show him to have lived elsewhere; the enumerator also recorded William Plane as resident in Grimwade's Cottages, not Peck Square as in the rate book. The inconsistent spelling of surnames is also, to say the least, another source of confusion (*see* the occupant of 'No. 4' and of the 'House and Shop'). Furthermore, the different listings suggest that the occupants of houses changed quite frequently, and that must have presented considerable difficulties for enumerators, rating officers and the compilers of directories as they went about their work (as well as for the historian of the 20th century!).

Public Health

Another source, invaluable for the study of urban housing, including working-class areas, is the Annual Report of the Medical Officer of Health. Such reports should be available in local record offices. Their importance for the student can be illustrated by two extracts for Ipswich [**33** & **34**], which give specific instances of fevers and infectious outbreaks, dampness and the lack of through-ventilation in houses, the proximity of 'closets' and 'foul soil bins', open cesspits, blocked and broken drains, back-to-back houses, small courts, the subletting of rooms at high rents, overcrowding and the lack of adequate water-supplies.

It will be noted that these sources also refer to the legal framework of national legislation within which Medical Officers of Health acted (for example 'Cross's Acts' and 'Torrens Acts'). They also indicate the municipal bodies through which the M.O.H. argued his case for slum clearance (the Health Committee, the Nuisances Removal Committee and the Urban Sanitary Authority).

Local archives may reveal other sources for the study of public health and housing: for example, the reports of government inspectors on the sanitary condition of individual towns (we have two for Ipswich); the minute books of a town's Public Health Committee; local Registers of Deaths; and the writings of local social investigators like John Glyde of Ipswich. He, in 1850, published his *Moral, Social and Religious Condition of Ipswich*, which includes a description of crowded and unhealthy courts in the town [**35**].

Overcrowding in New Street, St Clements, Ipswich

It is a common practice in many parts of Ipswich to let off single rooms in old and dilapidated houses into weekly tenements. By so doing the proprietors evade coming under the Common Lodging Houses Act and are not compelled to observe the rules of cleanliness and cubical space which the Act requires. Families live, sleep, cook and wash in these rooms and are sometimes entirely without a water supply . . .

As a example of the large sums made by letting out furnished rooms to weekly tenants I may mention three houses in New Street, St Clements, belonging to the same proprietor. One, at the top of the street which is fairly constructed and well ventilated, and for which the person who sublets it pays £10 a year, was at the time of my visit, let out at the following rentals — the two front rooms on each side of the front door at 4/6 a week each, the rooms over at 3/6 each, and the kitchen at the back was occupied by a married couple at 4/- a week; the other rooms were not at that time let: in one of the upstairs rooms, occupied by a family of four, I found a case of Typhoid fever. The sanitary arrangements of the house were better than usual, but the cellar was half full of stagnant water . . . the other two houses were old and ill-ventilated cottages, sublet to five separate families, numbering in all 20 persons, at the following weekly rentals — 4/6, 4/6, 3/-, 3/-, 3/-, and yet the drain in the yard was blocked, which caused the foul sewage to soak through into the house in the next street . . . I must think that where houses are let out to a number of people at such high rentals, the landlords should see that their sanitary condition is better attended to.

33. Extract from an annual sanitary report: *First Annual Report on the Sanitary Condition of the Borough and Port of Ipswich*, by George Sampson Elliston, Medical Officer of Health (1874), pp. 20-1.

"Further large powers for dealing with insanitary dwellings are conferred on all Urban Sanitary Authorities by the Artizans and Labourers' Dwellings Improvement Acts, 1875 to 1885, commonly known as Cross's Acts." "These Acts are, in fact, intended to enable Urban Sanitary Authorities to deal on a large scale with similar evils to those which Torrens' Acts are designed to cope on a small scale, and to afford a remedy in cases where the mischief to be cured is not such as can be effectually met by proceedings against individual owners in respect of particular houses, but where what is required is a complete scheme for the re-arrangement and re-construction of the streets and houses."

From these extracts it will be seen with what large powers Urban Sanitary Authorities have been invested with a view to enabling them to improve the sanitary conditions of the dwellings of the labouring classes, and they seem to be just what is wanted in dealing with that old standing nuisance, Long Lane, St Clement's.

A few months ago this Lane again came under the notice of the Health Committee, a death from Typhoid Fever having been registered in a house in Trinity Square, Long Lane, and a few weeks after a young man was reported to be lying ill in the same house with the same fever. He was at once removed to the Fever Hospital, and the house, which was badly situated in the corner of the square close to the closets and without through ventilation,

(continued opposite)

was closed within a week by order of the Health Committee as unfit for human habitation. It was understood by the Committee that I was about to report upon the sanitary condition of Long Lane, and I now take this opportunity of reporting upon it, as an area requiring improvement, direct to the Sanitary Authority.

It may be well here to give a brief history of Long Lane and the various schemes that have been proposed for its demolition and improvement. This Lane had long been looked upon as one of the nurseries for fever and epidemics in the Borough, the great epidemic of Small-pox in 1872, if it did not actually commence here, raged more virulently than in any other part of the town, and before the passing of the Public Health Act, 1875, I presented a report upon its condition to the Nuisances Removal Committee.

This report absolutely condemned sixteen houses as unfit for human habitation at the Back Hamlet end of the Lane, and an influential Committee was formed to visit the site, and a plan was prepared proposing to purchase the house on each side of the lane for demolition, and afterwards laying out a fresh street from Pottery Street to the end of Duke Street, and to sell off, lease, or rebuild on the surplus land . . .

When the plans were brought before the Council they rejected them all, but decided to purchase and pull down the sixteen condemned houses at a cost of £1,000, leaving the rest of the improvements to follow at some future date.

It is now fourteen years since these houses were demolished, and the open space thrown into the lane, the £1,000 was well laid out, for there has been no epidemic in this locality since, but in the meantime the houses that were left have been going from bad to worse; they have become so dilapidated, and so utterly wretched looking that a large number are tenantless, even the public-houses at each end have the same seedy and out-of-elbows look as the dwellings they adjoin.

I am of opinion that all the houses on the East side of the lane are more or less unfit for habitation. The four next the "Ship" have small back yards, the eight single houses in Trinity Square have lately been made more unwholesome by being built in by the Memorial Chapel in the Back Hamlet; they are also damp, ill-ventilated, and surrounded by closets and foul soil bins. The same description applies to the next six "single houses" and eight back to back houses, while the fourteen houses on the "carnser" stand sadly in the way of an improvement, they are small badly-built houses, with back premises in a very bad and dangerous condition, the soil bins being open cesspools, and the drainage blocked and broken. Anyhow these back premises must be demolished and re-constructed. On the west side of the Lane are sixteen houses, including two single houses in a small court, and four in Chapel Yard; they are not so bad as those on the east side, but the back yards are small, close, badly ventilated, with foul deep midden pits.

I trust the Sanitary Authority will take a broad view of the improvement, and in laying out a street 30 feet wide, purchase the property on either side, for I need hardly point out that in acquiring the houses and ground on both sides they not only reap the benefit of the improvement, but can afterwards regulate the class and number of dwellings to be erected on the surplus ground. In some continental towns, such as Brussels, where the Municipality have carried out street improvements on an enormous scale, the surplus ground has been sold off or leased so as nearly to recoup the original outlay . . .

34. Extract from an annual sanitary report: *Twelfth Annual Report on the Sanitary Condition of the Borough and Port of Ipswich*, by George Sampson Elliston, Medical Officer of Health (1889), pp. 20-2.

There are 106 courts in the town, containing 627 houses. The drainage from some of these is very defective. In some instances all the refuse water has to be carried to a dead well, situated either in the middle or at the end of the yard. In others, the water course is very badly paved, and stagnant water is the consequence. The demoralizing practice of providing but one convenience for several houses is here seen in full force. No less than 67 courts, containing 358 houses, are in this position; giving an average of one to every five houses. The courts are also equally deficient in accommodation for the washing of clothes. Many of the inhabitants have to perform that operation in their dwellings, to the serious injury of their health and destruction of their comfort. The supply of water to the courts is also of a defective character. Ten of them are without any supply, to 4 the water they require is fetched from wells, and to 21 from pumps. The difficulty and the labour attending the procuration of this needful article, must have a deteriorating influence on the character of the inhabitants, and prevent the formation of those habits of cleanliness so essential to the health, comfort, and moral elevation of the poorer classes. The ventilation of the courts is bad, their situation often very confined, and the entrance in some instances narrow. Some of their houses are situated back to back. Above 500 of them have no back doors; and, in the major portion, the rooms are so small that, where they are occupied by families, they cannot fail of being *crowded* in the sleeping apartments.

35. Contemporary description of insanitary courts, taken from John Glyde, *Moral, Social and Religious Condition of Ipswich* (1850), p. 36.

36. Contemporary description of an urban family, extracted from A. Fried & R. Elman (eds.), *Charles Booth's London* (1969), p. 125.

No. 2 Parker Street has two entrances, the one being numbered at 159 Drury Lane. One of the parlour floors is used for the sale of coal and coke, and the room over for living in . . . . in one of those rooms there was at one time a Mrs Carter, a woman with a fiery temper, almost fit to commit murder, and her husband has been in prison for ill-using her. She was, however, a clean, hard-working woman. These people were at times very poor. On the second floor to the right there were a man and a woman (English) who had lived unmarried for fourteen years. There were no children; the room clean, with a few comforts. In the other room lived another pair in the same fashion; the woman very unhappy, brutally treated by the man, whom she says she would leave if she knew how else to get a living. Such cases are not uncommon. The man was a drunkard. On the third floor lived an old woman and her son, Irish, who declined to be visited by a Protestant missionary.

'Biographies'

In spite of their listed and statistical form, the descriptions of households in enumerators' books have much human interest, and could be used to write biographies and short family histories. Here, for example, are details for some Ipswich families which cry out for interpretation in the form of continuous prose (remember that the year is 1881):

No. 42 Long Lane

Joseph Bartlett	Head	M	42	Labourer	Plymouth
Harriett Bartlett	Wife	M	35		Ipswich
Joseph Bartlett	Son		16	Foundry Apprentice	Plymouth
William Bartlett	Son		14	Foundry Apprentice	Alderney
Henry Bartlett	Son		13	Scholar	Dublin
Mary Bartlett	Dau		9		East India
Sarah Bartlett	Dau		7		East India
Halford Bartlett	Son		4		Ipswich
Charles Bartlett	Son		2		Ipswich

Short Lane

William Twaite	Head	M	37	Bricklayer	Roydon, Norfolk
Mary A. Twaite	Wife	M	38		Scotland
Jane A. Johnson	Step-dau		9		Scotland
Agnes Johnson	Step-dau		7		Scotland
Ellen B. Twaite	Dau		3		Scotland
Francis Twaite	Dau		3		Scotland
William Twaite	Son		1		Scotland
[Un-named]	Dau		14 days		Ipswich

Sometimes the human relationships are more difficult to unravel:

No. 5 Short Lane

Alice Caley	Head	W	57	Charwoman	Ipswich
Alice Hines	Dau	U	38	Charwoman	Ipswich
Frederick Caley	Son	U	32	Labourer	Ipswich
Elvina Caley	Dau	U	28	Staymaker	Ipswich
Emily Caley	Dau	U	20	Staymaker	Ipswich
Jane Caley	Dau	U	15	Boot Fitter	Ipswich
Alice Hines	Grand-dau		7	Scholar	East India
Kate Caley	Grand-dau		2		Ipswich

What different interpretations can be put forward for the Caley family?

In doing work of this kind, our students would be following in famous footsteps. For example, Charles Booth, when investigating London's slums in the 1880s, used different sources and his own personal interviews to build up fascinating 'biographies' of families in whole streets [**36**].

Although students could not write such a 'biography' from the census alone, they might be able to find and exploit other sources about individual families to build up a fuller picture. Here is one example which uses the census entry for No. 28 Long Lane, Ipswich, with the rate book, the burial register for St Helen's parish, and a report on proceedings in a police court from a local newspaper called *The Suffolk Chronicle* (such reports of petty crimes appear regularly):

CENSUS, 3 April 1881

No. 28 Long Lane

Eliza Horne	Head	23	Sailor's wife	born	Ipswich
Elvina Horne	Dau.	7 mo.		,,	Ipswich
Elaine Sheldrake	Mother, Wid.	47		,,	Debenham [Suffolk]
Emily Sheldrake	Dau.	9		,,	Debenham [Suffolk]

BURIAL REGISTER, St HELEN'S, IPSWICH, 11 February 1881

Elijah Sheldrake, aged 49, of Long Lane

RATE BOOK, Lady Day, 1881

Occupier: Elijah Sheldrake [crossed out] Herbert Horne [inserted]

THE SUFFOLK CHRONICLE, 6 August 1881

Ipswich Police Court, Thursday, August 4th, before the Deputy Mayor (D. H. Booth, Esq.), G. G. Sampson, Esq., and Admiral Mason, C.B.

ROBBING A BROTHER — George Sheldrake, Long Lane, was charged with stealing a purse and £4 in money, the property of his brother, Samuel Sheldrake, naval seaman on board H.M.S. Adelaide, Prosecutor said he came home from Plymouth on Wednesday 3rd of August, to see his mother. Just before dinner he went out with prisoner to get some beer at the 'Ocean Queen'. Whilst there he gave his watch and purse to his little sister, who was with them, to keep — Emily Sheldrake said she went with her brothers to the 'Ocean Queen'. Her brother Samuel gave her his watch and purse to keep. Soon afterwards her brother George asked her for the purse. She gave it to him, and he took some money from it and then handed it back. When she took it home she told her mother what her brother George had done — Police Sergeant Garnham said he searched prisoner and found £2 19s. upon him. On asking prisoner where he got it, he said all the money he had he earned by hard work — the Magistrate committed prisoner to take his trial at the next Quarter Sessions. Bail was allowed, two sureties in £10, and himself in £10.

On the basis of this evidence, the 'history' of the Horne and Sheldrake families could be analysed and written up — perhaps from the point of view of Emily Sheldrake?

Vice and virtue

If time and sources allow, another fascinating and wider aspect of local life could be investigated. For example, the town plan and census reveal that at least seven public houses lay within two hundred yards of Long Lane, Ipswich. On the other hand, that same street had a Working Men's Library at one end, and a Working Men's Institute at the other, as well as a Congregational Chapel and a Sunday School. Thus, one of the great themes of Victorian history is opened up for the class to discuss and investigate: the Demon Drink *versus* Moral and Mental Improvement.

Poverty

Students might even be encouraged to test aspects of Social Theory. Can they find out how many families/households in their area were likely to have been in poverty, bearing in mind the limitations of their evidence and remembering the theory of a 'cycle of poverty' which was developed by social commentators like Charles Booth and Seebohm Rowntree?

When a young man first got married, and during the early months of married life while his wife was probably earning, he enjoyed a modest standard of comfort, but when his children began to multiply and his wife could no longer earn, he was very likely to fall into poverty. By middle age his children would become young wage earners and the family economy would improve. But with old age came a renewed time of hardship as his health and strength began to fail.

By looking carefully at census entries, students should be able to find local cases which might illustrate the 'cycle of poverty'. This would naturally lead to a classroom discussion of the work of these two great Victorian social scientists.

IV

STUDY AREA 2: A CENTRAL SHOPPING STREET

The main concern of this section is to suggest ways of studying the commercial area of a large town. Again, the intention is to develop both analytical skills and an understanding of the processes of continuity and change. By exploiting a wide range of sources, students should be able not only to describe the economic environment of a major shopping street at a single point in time, in and after 1881, but to trace the main stages of its development over a longer period, both physically and economically.

The essential questions which need to be put to the evidence, when studying change in a shopping street, may be listed as follows:

1881
What was the population of the street in 1881?
What different trades and occupations did the inhabitants follow?
How many shops did the street contain?
Did the street contain any private houses in 1881?
Who were the resident occupants of private houses?
Which tradesmen were resident in the street?
Did the street contain any industrial sites?
Is there evidence of large companies or stores, rather than family businesses?
What evidence is there of the physical appearance of the street in the early 1880s?

1881 to present: economic change
What is the (estimated?) population of the street today?
What is the pattern of shops in the street at present?
What changes in the pattern can be detected between 1881 and the present?
When did major changes take place?

1881 to present: changes in townscape
How has the architecture and layout of the street changed from the 1880s to the
   present day?
When did the greatest physical changes take place?
What documentary as well as physical evidence helps to explain the changes?
What general conclusions can be drawn by comparing the street in 1881 with the
   street today?

The variety of sources, particularly visual ones, will provide many opportunities for different lines of enquiry. If specific questions are asked, and stress is put on accurate analysis and logical presentation of the findings, students should be able to develop and use a number of different skills. They should be encouraged to keep a careful note

37. Part of the town plan of Ipswich, 10.56 feet to one mile, 1881, showing Carr Street and its surroundings.

of their procedures and sources, so that they can support their conclusions with properly presented evidence. They must be careful about making assumptions if the evidence does not offer clear proof: the question always in their minds must be, 'How far can I draw conclusions from this evidence, and how can I accurately express those conclusions?'.

The street in 1881: finding our whereabouts

The following example, using the four key sources, could be used to show the steps that can be taken to locate a particular section of street, and to relate the households in the census to the sites depicted on the town plan. By introducing each source in turn, the teacher can raise questions and point out the way in which problems can be tackled. This exercise relates to that section of Carr Street in Ipswich which runs from 'Cox Lane' to 'Major's Corner'.

Start with the town plan [37]. What evidence helps us to establish which section of the street is being referred to? (In fact, only Major's Corner at the east end of the street is specifically located.) Of the turnings off Carr Street, which is Cox Lane, and on which side of the street is it?

Now look at the directory [38]. The statements 'here is Cox Lane' and 'here is Major's Corner' suggest that the relevant sites run from No. 48 to No. 72. Note, however, that the numbering is not in strict sequence: should No. 68 be included in place of No. 72 or not? Until we have other points of reference, we cannot be certain about this, or whether the sites are on the north or south side of the street. However, if students spot the reference to *Cross Keys* in the directory, and the fact that the plan shows this public house on the south side, they can resolve the latter point. Thus, given the numbering of the entries, Cox Lane must lie halfway between the *Cross Keys* and Major's Corner, and the particular sites under investigation must run from No. 48 to Major's Corner.

Having located the section on the plan, turn now to the list of heads of households extracted from the enumerator's book [39]. First, the sequence of house numbers confirms that the directory is misprinted, and that No. 68 should be included, and not No. 72. The next step is to try to relate the buildings depicted on the plan to the households in the census, but another problem immediately arises. The census and directory both list 12 households or occupiers, but the plan only shows 11 buildings abutting the street! The rate book, which can now be brought into play [40], also lists only 11 occupiers and properties. How can this discrepancy be resolved?

Look now at the house numbers in both census and directory. According to the census, No. 62 has two occupants, 'Frances Fish' and 'Isaac Harvey'. The directory lists 'Fish, Fk & Son, cabinet and upholstery works' and 'Harvey, Isaac'. In the rate book, this property is described as owned and occupied by Frederick Fish, and consisting of 'House Buildings Stables and yard'. Its description and valuation of £90 define it clearly as the large site marked on the plan. Therefore, it can be presumed that Isaac Harvey, described as 'coachman' in the census and 'groom' in the directory, lived in the yard (possibly over the stables). Note, too, that Frederick Fish himself was actually absent on the night of the census. Thus the problem is solved by a careful examination of the evidence, and the occupants of the 11 houses in the block can be satisfactorily located.

Cole Wm. merchants' clerk
Turner Wm. grocers' assistant
Ambrose John, tobacconist
Mayhew Hy. Board of Works assistant
9 Westrop Hy. grocers' assistant
10 Gosling Hy. serjeant, Militia

West Villa

Jackson Mrs.
Vacant
Cookson O. A.
Eastaugh John
Steel Miss
Tween Mrs. 2, Alpine lodge
Wray John, 1 do.

here is Cumberland street

CARDINAL STREET
FRIARS ROAD.

1 Hunt Wm. E. railway porter
2 Frost Mrs laundress
3 Rose Miss, furrier
4 Horn Mrs. laundress
5 McLeod Geo. tailor
6 Diggins Wm. coal carter
7 Mann James
8 Halls Walter, mariner
9 Pyett Wm. police constable
10 Wright Walter. labourer
11 Youngs Henry, cabinetmaker
12 Dennis Mrs. E.
13 Spooner Wm. carriage fitter
14 Bedwell J. G. labourer
15 Punchard Mrs
16 Nunn Chas. police constable
17 Whistle Mrs. E. laundress
18 Reeve John, timekeeper
19 Barnes Mrs. dressmaker
20 Newson Thomas, soapmaker
21 Diggins Wm. coal carter
22 Lorking Mrs. W. laundress
Watson Wm. beerseller

here is Cecilia street

Pollard F. contractor, &c
Moss H. D. builder, &c

CARDINAL STREET NEW
COMMERCIAL ROAD.

Smyth E. boot & shoemaker
1 Ratcliffe John, labourer
2 Turvey Josh, railway ticket collector

3 Bishop Henry, railway ticket collector
4 Long John, acting goods guard
5 Harding H. J. railway clerk
6 Liddle Robert, railway goods clerk
7 Scrivener Geo. baker
8 Spark Hy. railway porter
9 Pratt D. railway porter
10 Lamb T. W. junr. compositor
11 Lamb T. W. senr. blacksmith

here is Quadling street

Hines Wm. baker, &c
1 Cross F. ostler
2 Finch Ewd. Chas. rlwy. guard
3 Grimwood Chas. engine driver
4 Cutting Elias, engine fitter
5 Porter Walter, police constable
6 Cole Geo. railway shunter
7 Gentry Geo. boiler maker
8 Walker Jas. carpenter
9 Vacant
10 do.
11 do.
12 do.

CARR STREET
TAVERN ST., NORTHGATE ST. AND UPPER BROOK STREET.

1 & 3 Younger R. E. chemist, oil and colour warehouseman
5 Cook J. W. confectioner, &c
7 Aldous Ewl. hatter & hosier
9 Clark Miss M. Modes-de-Paris
11 Howe T.P., M.C.P.

here is Little Colman street

13 Edwards G. C. surgeon and apothecary
15 Norbrook Mrs
17 *East Anglian Daily Times* office
17 *Suffolk Times & Mercury* office
19 Massingham Geo. grocer, &c
21 Ipswich Nurses' Home—Miss ——, lady superintendent
23 Ansill Thos. baker, &c
25 Ward Robt. wood turner, &c
27 Wright Jeaffreson, boot maker
29 Pierce Mrs
31a Pells John Clarke

31 Pells John & Sons, builders, contractors, brick and timber merchants
33 Davis Mrs. Preparatory School
35 & 37 Godball Joseph, music warehouse
39 Crane Geo. Joseph, carver and guilder
41 Titchmarsh Fk.
43 & 45 Reeve A. tea & coffee house
47 Stewart Chas. boot and shoe manufacturer
49 & 51 Fenn Wm. Ar. *Salutation Inn*
53 Bevan Chas. butcher
55 Baker Miss, fancy draper
57 Bead Jas. watch & clockmaker
59 Grimwood Thos. corn, hay and straw dealer

here is Old Foundry road

68 Burch Geo. furniture dealer

here is Majors corner

72 Churchyard G. dining and refreshment rooms
66 Ralph C. fish dealer
64 Beecraft Walter, beer retailer
62 Fish Miss
62a Harvey Isaac. groom
Fish Fk. & Son, cabinet and upholstery works
60 Vacant
58 Eade Wm. architect & surveyor
56 Barber Samuel. baker, &c.
54 Greatrex Fk. collar and saddle maker
52 Johnson Mrs E. bootmaker
50 Greenmass F. G. newsagent,&c
48 Withers W. R. muffin & crumpit baker

here is Cox lane

46 Knights R. shoeing and general smith
44 Vacant
42 Ipswich Industrial Co-operative Society
40 do
38 Smith Thos. Dudley, haircutter
36 Tibbenham John, carver and gilder
32 Harrison H. D. auctioneer, valuer, house agent, &c
30 Morse Fk.

28 Cross Wm. brewers labourer
26 Freston Mrs. E. *Cross Keys*
24 & 22 Scheuermann Geo. butcher
20 Cracknall R. boot & shoemaker, &c
18 Topham W. J. watchmaker, &c
15 & 14 Clover J. C. greengrocer &c
12 Thrower Mrs. general shop
10 Love Wm. fruiterer and confectioner
8 Carrington B. poulterer & game dealer
8 Carrington Mrs registry office for servants
6 Brereton H. A. fruiterer, greengrocer and waiter
4 & 2 Pick G. T. general draper &c

CASTLE STREET
STIRLING STREET.

1 Burman Peter, gardener
3 Poole Chas. boot closer
5 Gooch Robt. carpenter
7 Parker Robt. labourer
9 Ellis Geo. carter
11 Turtill Robt. boot closer
13 Pulham W. railway porter
15 Cullum Geo.
17 Bacon Ben. boot & shoemaker
19 Pulham Chas. cooper
21 Ward Chas. telegraph engineer
23 Turner Robt. carpenter
25 Kamp H. general shop
27 Barnard V. chair maker and repairer
20 Knight Robt. railway carman

here is Perth street

4 Pooley Joseph, marine store dealer

CAVENDISH STREET
FORE HAMLET.

Gibbons E. & E. C. brick makers, &c

1 Frith Wm. foundry labourer
2 Warren Wm. foundry labourer
3 Battell W. carpenter
4 Quinton Henry, foundry smith
5 Longhurst Wm. timekeeper
6 Sporle Wm. mariner
7 Green Wm
8 Kettle Wm. carpenter
9 Keeble Anthony, gas labourer

38. Extract from a directory: *Steven's Directory of Ipswich and Neighbourhood* (1881), pp. 95-6.

This example may appear rather laboured, but detailed, accurate, step-by-step procedures of this kind are fundamental to historical research, and their value must be stressed to students. It is not simply a matter of locating households, but of learning the historian's critical and analytical methods: not guesswork but logical procedure.

48	William Withers	Muffin Maker
50	Frederick Greengrass	Tailors cutter/Newsagent & Tobacconist
52	Elizabeth Johnson	Shoemaker
54	Frederick Greatrex	Saddler & Collar Maker
56	Samuel Barber	Dairyman
58	William Eade	Architect & Surveyor
60	Frederick Barker	Accountant
62	Isaac Harvey	Coachman
62	Frances Fish	House keeper
64	Walter Beecroft	'Race Horse'
66	Ralph Carrington	Fishmonger
68	George Burch	Ironplate worker

39. Details extracted from a census enumerator's book, 1881: heads of households living in Nos. 48-68 Carr Street, Ipswich, with their occupations.

Name of Occupier	Name of Owner	Description	Gross Estimated Rental	Rateable Value
			£. s. d.	£. s. d.
George Burch	M. Upson	House & yard	7. 0. 0	5.17. 6
Carrington Ralph	M. Upson	House & yard	14. 5. 0	12.10. 0
Walter Beecroft	M. Upson	Beer House & yard	26. 0. 0	22. 0. 0
Frederick Fish	F. Fish	House Buildings Stables & yard	100. 0. 0	90. 0. 0
Frederick Barker	S. P. Closson	House & Garden	40. 0. 0	34. 0. 0
William Eade	W. Cattermole	House Buildings & Garden	30. 0. 0	26. 0. 0
Samuel Barber	L. T. Clements	House Bake Office & yard	26. 0. 0	23. 0. 0
Frederick Greatrex	I. Pells	House & yard	10.10. 0	9. 5. 0
Johnson	I. Pells	House & yard	10. 0. 0	8.10. 0
Frederick Geo. Greengrass	I. Pells	House & yard	12. 0. 0	10.10. 0
William Withers	I. Pells	House & yard	10.10. 0	9. 0. 0

40. Transcript of a rate book, 1881, for the parish of St Margaret's, Ipswich, showing details for part of Carr Street.

Nos. 5-9 Carr Street

The analysis of particular households, using the enumerators' books, directories and rate books, offers opportunities for the use of both interpretative skills and imagination. Having extracted and weighed the evidence, students can be encouraged to write short 'biographies' of chosen households. The following examples of assembled evidence show some of the possibilities, by using entries for Nos. 5-9 Carr Street:

No. 5 Carr Street
Census: inhabited by Hannah M. Cattermole, unmarried, aged 48, with 'income from 6 cottages', born in Ipswich
Directory: Cook, J. W., confectioner &c
Rate Book: Occupier, James Wells Cook
                     Owner, J. R. Cattermole

Conclusions: Miss Cattermole, a woman of independent means, a property owner, lived at No. 5, which was presumably owned by a relative. She probably lived above the shop, which was a confectioner's. The tenant of the shop, not resident according to the census, was Mr. Cook.

No. 7 Carr Street
Census: unoccupied
Directory: Aldous, Edward, hatter & hosier
Rate Book: Occupier, Edward Aldous
                        Owner, J. R. Cattermole

Conclusions: The shopkeeper either was not resident on the night of the census, had a private residence elsewhere, or had vacated the tenancy since the rate book had been made up.

No. 9 Carr Street
Census: Mary Clarke, unmarried, aged 48, a dressmaker, lived here. She had, living
                        in, one assistant aged 38 called Ellen Goodrum, and a servant girl aged 16
                        called Alice Long.
Directory: Clark, Miss M., Modes-de-Paris
Rate Book: Occupier, Mary Clarke
                        Owner, J. R. Cattermole

Conclusions: A dressmaker's shop run by a middle-aged spinster. Work was produced by Miss Clarke and her assistant. They lived above the shop with one servant. The name of the shop suggests a genteel clientele. Were Parisian fashions popular at this date? Was Miss Clarke 'trendy'?

N.B. The rate book shows that all these properties were owned by the same man. Can they be located on the plan?

Small-scale exercises along these lines will give students excellent practice in historical interpretation and writing, before they tackle more demanding projects. Indeed, such work could easily be accumulated and extended to build up the detailed human profile of a whole street. Other sources might easily be deployed such as advertisements for businesses in newspapers and directories, early photographs and recorded reminiscences.

The Co-op store

By the late-19th century, most shopping streets in the centres of towns and cities contained examples of large departmental stores. This development offers interesting possibilities for study. In Ipswich in 1881, Nos. 38-42 Carr Street housed the Ipswich Co-operative Society [5]. In 1885 the store, until then housed in converted buildings, was completely rebuilt: an imposing building which still dominates the south-eastern end of the street. In 1886 a local newspaper celebrated the official opening by describing the history of the co-operative movement in Ipswich. Meanwhile the Society itself published a commemorative pamphlet which, amongst other fascinating information, included this architect's drawing [41] and a detailed description of the layout of the store's interior, its departments, public rooms and offices [42]. The opening of such large stores, of chapels and churches, of public and commercial buildings, was usually reported in the local press, giving much detail about leading figures and about the social, religious, civic or economic significance of new developments in the life of the town.

New Central Stores for the Ipswich Industrial Co-operative Society. James F Goodey Archt Colchester.

THE NEW BUILDINGS

are in the form of a gnomon, with a total frontage of 210 feet. The front is of white brick and concrete dressings. The mean height of the building is 60 feet. Beneath the whole building are spacious cellars for storage. On the ground floor are seven separate shops, viz., grocery, boots and shoes, men's and boys' outfitting, drapery, hardware and furnishing, and two butchers' shops, all excellently fitted up with mahogany and pitch pine, the walls and ceilings being match-boarded, except the butchers' which have glazed brick walls. On the first floor are the Manager's and Secretary's offices, which are well-fitted and furnished. Adjoining is the reading-room and library, a pleasant neatly-furnished room, measuring 34 feet by 25 feet. Next comes a room measuring 33 feet by 35 feet, which is intended for a furniture show-room; and adjoining is a drapery showroom, which is rather larger. Further on is another large room, also intended to be a showroom, and at the end of the building are two bedrooms, a keeping-room, and kitchen for the use of the caretaker. On the second, or top floor, is the large hall, to be called the Co-operative Hall, which will comfortably seat 800 persons. Nearly 1,200 crowded into it, however, for a recent political meeting. It is by far the handsomest hall in the town, and second in size, and is expected to be in great requisition for concerts and other meetings. Every convenience has been arranged for holding large tea meetings, etc. On the same floor is a smaller hall, which will hold about 200 persons, and will be used for members' monthly meetings, and also let if required. Convenient ante-rooms are attached to both halls. Mr. J. F. Goodey, of Colchester, has been the architect, and Mr. F. Dupont, of the same town, the builder. The whole building has been admirably arranged, and the work is well done.

41. Architect's drawing of a new store, 1886: depicting the new premises of the Ipswich Co-operative Society, completed that year, from 'Opening Celebration of the New Central Stores, 26 April 1886', in *Eastern Counties Gazette.*

42. A contemporary description of a new store: from 'Opening Celebration of the New Central Stores, 26 April 1886', in *Eastern Counties Gazette.*

Local organisations often celebrated later stages of their history and anniversaries by producing other publications, copies of which may well survive in record offices or still remain in the hands of the organisation itself. For instance, in 1928 the Ipswich Co-operative Society published a booklet, which covers its history *Through Sixty Years* in some detail and gives short biographies of leading figures in the local movement. One William Beverley is described thus:

> Mr William Beverley was one of the original members of the Society, joining in March, 1868. He was born at Burnham Market, in Norfolk, and coming to Ipswich, he followed the trade of harness maker. Joining the Committee of the Society in 1872 he undertook the secretarial work in his spare time. This he did until 1877, when he was appointed full-time Secretary. In 1883 the secretary ceased to be a member of the Committee, and Mr Beverley became a paid official without the powers of a committee-man. Apparently he lived on the premises, for we learn that Mrs Beverley occasionally helped to make pork cheese for the butcher. Mr Beverley resigned in 1896, and after a few years' stay in Ipswich he returned to his native place at Burnham Market, but he did not live very long to enjoy his well-earned rest. His death occurred in September, 1909.

In the census, sure enough (not 'apparently', as the booklet says), we find William Beverley living at the Co-op premises in Carr Street with his wife Harriett and daughter Kate, who was a dressmaker. The store also had a resident butcher, Philip Webb, living at No. 42 with his wife and two daughters. The latter were draper's assistants, as was a female boarder. Philip Webb was clearly the butcher with whom Mrs. Beverley worked 'to make pork cheese'. (What, incidentally, is 'pork cheese'?) Webb's daughters probably worked in the drapery department of the store.

Thus, the Co-op's commemorative booklet not only gives a very useful summary of the movement's development over 60 years, but provides vital evidence about individuals which, when related to other sources, helps to expand the possibilities of re-creating and re-populating a street. If a class were studying the Co-operative Movement nationally, then local sources such as these would provide excellent case studies for individual towns.

Reminiscences

Your record office or library may also hold magazines or journals which, if indexed, could yield more evidence about streets and shops. Thus, The *East Anglian Magazine* of July 1951 contained the reminiscences of a man, L. J. Tibbenham, whose father lived at No. 34 Carr Street in 1881. Tibbenham himself appears in the census as a child aged two, and his recollections of a slightly later period contain a wealth of information about the street. His comments provide vivid evidence of the street's character in the 1880s, and could be tested against the census of 1881 [43].

Testimony like Tibbenham's could be tested against both the census and the directory of 1881, for he has a lot to say about particular shops:

> There was quite a variety of shops in this street of ours. There was the wood turner's. He had all kinds of turned pieces of wood in the window. There was a harness shop, a very essential shop, for this was a horsy period. There was the newspaper printing works, the beginning of the *East Anglian Daily Times*. If I woke up in the night I could always hear the roar of the printing presses. And, near the harness shop, was a newspaper shop. It was a very tiny place. I was always horrified by the

sheets displayed outside the window. They always seemed to show murders, fires, earthquakes and all kinds of dreadful things. Whether they really happened I do not know. Inside the shop was the usual collection of penny dreadfuls which were all the rage at that time and every February the most grotesque Valentines were sold by the yard.

His description of a 'crumpet man' or 'muffin man' and his father is particularly evocative in its detail:

> He would be about the streets quite early crying, 'hot crumpets'. He had a bell and he carried a board on his head. It was supported on a green baize ring like a cushion. The crumpet man's father used to make rock. He was a big fellow with curly hair and a bald patch in front. He had great brawny arms and he used to throw the rock over a hook attached to the wall of his shop which we could see from our front window . . .

At No. 48 Carr Street, the census of 1881 obligingly lists William Withers, aged 50, 'Muffin Maker'. Once again, the cross reference is very useful for elaborating the bare

---

I Remember The Crumpet Man

Carr Street, the main street of Ipswich, was not 60 years ago the shopping centre that it is today, but a very narrow thoroughfare mostly made up of private houses with a few shops dotted about in between.

The street twisted like a snake and the roadway was of stones and was always dirty . . .

The narrowness of the street will be obvious when I say that one of my elder brothers was very expert with a peashooter and he used to blow peas from our attic window across to the windows opposite . . .

Gradually, as the years went by the street took on a new shape. I should think more than half of it was pulled down and rebuilt in its present form. My father was always talking about it but I never realised what was taking place. All I know is that we were lucky and that my father's little house was one of the few places left. I saw the Lyceum Theatre built. I saw the site cleared and a large hole dug out for its pit and after its short life I saw it demolished . . .

Adjoining the alleyway of the Cross Keys was a very large house, half-timbered and surrounded at the back by a 10 foot wall. I remember it very well because it came up to our back yard and shut out every bit of sunlight. For some time, I recall, the house was occupied by a very fashionable doctor who used to drive out with a pair of high-stepping greys.

Another half-timbered building was the shop at Cox Lane corner where the man made his rock. It had a wonderful corner post. In later years, when alterations were being made to the street, this building was purchased, or at least the woodwork, by my brother. We little thought, my brothers and I, when we used to watch the brawny, perspiring man making his rock, that one of us would one day buy the old place. I believe the old house was reconstructed and re-erected elsewhere, perhaps in the United States, as a genuine old English timbered house.

---

43. An example of recorded reminiscences: note particularly the references to the street's narrow, twisting nature, the rebuilding of 'nearly half' of it, and the building of the Lyceum Theatre (in fact in 1890). Taken from 'I Remember the Crumpet Man, the Rock Maker and the old Horse Tram', by L. J. Tibbenham, in *East Anglian Magazine*, Vol. 10, No. 11 (July, 1951), pp. 678-85.

detail of the census entry and, once again, the trade will need to be explained. Document **44** is Henry Mayhew's description of it, one amongst many of his fascinating explorations of street trades in Victorian times. This example, as with others already discussed, could be the starting point for classwork on this aspect of the economic life of 19th-century towns.

Of Muffin and Crumpet-Selling in the Streets

The street-sellers of muffins and crumpets rank among the old street-tradesmen. It is difficult to estimate their numbers, but they were computed for me at 500, during the winter months. They are for the most part boys, young men, or old men, and some of them infirm. There are a few girls in the trade, but very few women.

The ringing of the muffin-man's bell — attached to which the pleasant associations are not a few — was prohibited by a recent Act of Parliament, but the prohibition has been as inoperative as that which forbade the use of a drum to the costermonger, for the muffin bell still tinkles along the streets, and is rung vigorously in the suburbs.

I did not hear of any street-seller who made the muffins or crumpets he vended. Indeed, he could not make the small quantity required, so as to be remunerative. The muffins are bought of the bakers, and at prices to leave a profit of 4d. in 1s. Some bakers give thirteen to the dozen to the street-sellers whom they know. The muffin-man carries his delicacies in a basket, wherein they are well swatched in flannel, to retain the heat: 'People likes them warm, sir,' an old man told me, 'to satisfy them they're fresh, and they almost always *are* fresh; but it can't matter so much about their being warm, as they have to be toasted again. I only wish good butter was a sight cheaper, and that would make the muffins go. Butter's half the battle.'

A sharp London lad of fourteen, whose father had been a man baker, and whose mother (a widow) kept a small chandler's shop, gave me the following account:-

'I turns out with muffins and crumpets, sir, in October, and continues until it gets well into spring, according to the weather. I carries a fust-rate article; werry much so. If you was to taste 'em, sir, you'd say the same. If I sells three dozen muffins at ½d. each, and twice that in crumpets, it's a werry fair day, werry fair; all beyond that is a *good* day. The profit on the three dozen and the others is 1s., but that's a great help, really a wonderful help, to mother, for I should be only mindin' the shop at home. Perhaps I clears 4s. a week, perhaps more, perhaps less; but that's about it, sir. Some does far better than that, and some can't hold a candle to it. If I has a hextra day's sale, mother'll give me 3d. to go to the play, and that hencourages a young man, you know, sir. If there's any unsold, a coffee-shop gets them cheap, and puts 'em off cheap again next morning. My best customers is genteel houses, 'cause I sells a genteel thing. I likes wet days best, 'cause there's werry respectable ladies what don't keep a servant, and they buys to save themselves going out. We're a great conwenience to the ladies, sir — a great conwenience to them as likes a slap-up tea. I *have* made 1s. 8d. in a day; that was my best. I once took only 2½d. — I don't know why — that was my worst. The shops don't love me — I puts their noses out.

---

44. A contemporary description of a street trade: from P. Quennell (ed.), *Mayhew's London* (1969), pp. 140-1.

45. **Advertisement** from Pawsey & Hayes, *Illustrated Guide to Ipswich* (1890), p. 156.

46. **Advertisement** from Pawsey & Hayes, *Almanack & Companion for Ipswich and Suffolk* (1890), p. xvi.

ESTABLISHED 1860.

G., A., & S. DIXEY,

WHOLESALE AND RETAIL FISHMONGERS,

9, KING STREET

(Opposite the New Corn Exchange), and at

66, CARR STREET, IPSWICH.

A Fresh Supply of Fish from all parts Daily.

G., A., and S. D. have made arrangements with Messrs. Johnstone and Sons, of Montrose, for the supply of Salmon daily during the season.

Orders to be Addressed : 9, KING STREET, IPSWICH.

ESTABLISHED 1844.

47.   Advertisement from Pawsey & Hayes, *Almanack & Companion for Ipswich and Suffolk* (1890), p. 55.

WHILLIER'S

MUSIC STORES.

SPECIAL AGENT FOR

CHAPPELL'S

AND OTHER LEADING MAKERS'

PIANOS.

TUNINGS AND REPAIRS.

The Largest Stock of Sheet Music in the County.

The Latest Operas, Songs and Pieces as soon as published.

—— **Special Facilities for Teachers.** ——

ACCREDITED DEALER OF THE GRAMOPHONE CO. LTD.

NEW RECORDS

. . each month. . .

Every H. M. V. Record in the Catalogue in Stock.

31 CARR STREET, IPSWICH.   Telephone 556.

48.   Advertisement from Kelly's *Directory of Ipswich* (1926), p. v.

Advertisements

As a final example of extra sources that may be available in most towns, we should certainly not overlook advertisements in newspapers and directories. John Tibbenham's advert from a guide of 1890 [45] helps to explain what a 'carver and gilder' actually did. J. F. Candler's from an almanack of the same year [46] raises a number of questions: does the heading, '17 Years with Mr Kingdom, Tavern Street', and the announcement that his stock is 'now Complete', suggest that his business was newly established? (This might be checked from other sources.) Does his statement that he stocks 'electro-plated' goods indicate new processes in the making of jewellery? (It may be possible to find out when this technique was first developed.) And what were the 'Keepers' that he advertised? The advert of G. A. & S. Dixey [47] gives information about this fishmonger's origins ('Established 1860'). The fact that No. 66 Carr Street was a branch indicates that their business had expanded, and that its connections were nation-wide ('Fish from all parts Daily', and arrangements via Montrose 'for the supply of Salmon daily'). The

G. STOLLERY,
Family Grocer & Provision Merchant,
49, Carr Street, IPSWICH.

. . NOTED FOR . .

First=class Groceries and Provisions
OF THE BEST QUALITY.

SPECIALITIES:

TURNER'S NOTED BAKING POWDER, makes Cooking a pleasure, 10d. per pound. First made in 1856. Try it. Grandmother used it.
Also the Celebrated JOHN BRIGHT TEA, 1/4, 1/6, 1/8, 2/- & 2/6 per pound. So well-known for their strength and delicious flavour.

SPECIAL TERMS TO HOTELS AND INSTITUTIONS.
SUPPORT THE PRIVATE TRADER.

49. Advertisement from Kelly's *Directory of Ipswich* (1910), p. 106.

advert of Whillier's Music Stores [**48**] enables us to explore the wider theme of popular or mass culture — what sheet music would have been on sale in 1926? In his advert of 1910, G. Stollery, Family Grocer and Provision Merchant [**49**], perhaps hints at the pressures on a small shopkeeper from the proliferation of multiple stores: he asks customers to 'Support the Private Trader'.

Continuity and change in a shopping street

For an examination of changes which have taken place in a shopping street between 1881 and the present day, street directories are invaluable. The wealth of detail, however, can raise problems by its very bulk and because the numbering of buildings is not necessarily consistent. Nonetheless, if students approach the evidence with certain specific questions in mind, they should be able to achieve useful results.

A good starting point is to compare the shops listed in directories of different dates, for example 1881 and 1939 [**38** & **50**]. Or one could compare 1881 with the present day. On the south side of Carr Street, for example, 25 shops were listed in 1881, but only 13 in 1939; the same length of street in 1987 produced a count of 11 shops. Another noticeable difference is the dominance in recent decades of large stores, 'multiples' like the Co-op and Woolworths, and of large national retailers such as Currys, Dewhurst the butchers and Milletts the tailors — as compared with the small private traders of 1881.

Before the 1870s virtually all shops in large towns were small, individual, family businesses, providing locally produced 'quality' goods for the better-off. There were some exceptions, notably the co-operative societies which, from their humble origin in Rochdale in 1844, began to appear throughout the country. As they developed, these co-ops were the first shops to introduce modern methods of organisation and distribution, aimed at supplying mass markets. In 1855, for example, co-ops in Lancashire and Yorkshire established their own wholesale society, and nationally they often experimented with the opening of branch shops. Thus, in the large towns, they became the first of what we now call the 'multiples' or chain stores, that today dominate our High Streets and, since the 1950s, have developed into the supermarket chains.

These pioneering methods of retailing began to transform the pattern of high-street shopping when, in the 1870s, private businessmen started up large-scale organisations as limited companies. This was most noticeable in the food trade. Thus the old-style grocer began to decline, and a new type of retailer, operating a chain of stores, showrooms and other outlets from a central headquarters, began to take over the central shopping areas of large towns. For instance, Thomas Lipton in 1872 ran a one-man grocery shop, but by 1880 he had 245 branches. Other familiar names like Sainsburys, Woolworths, the Home and Colonial and the Maypole Dairy Company, all began in the late 19th century.

20 Perkins Alfd
21 Race Geo. Rt
22 English Chas. Fredk
.... here are Cecilia & New
          Cardinal sts ....

CARR STREET, Tavern street
to St. Helen's st. Map F 6.
     North side.
1 Slack Wm. confctnr
3 Irene Ltd. costumiers
3a, Hepworth Madame, hair-
    drssr
5 Hubbard A. & W. watch mkrs
7 Miller & Son, tailors
9 Freeman, Hardy & Willis Ltd.
    boot mkrs
11 Salisbury's, fancy goods
11a, Richards B. R. turf commis-
    sion agt
11b, Lennards' Ltd. boot mkrs
...... here is Little Colman st ......
13 **EAST ANGLIAN DAILY TIMES**
    (The East Anglian Daily
    Times Co. Limited, publishrs)
13 **SUFFOLK CHRONICLE & MER-**
    CURY (The East Anglian
    Daily Times Co. Limited,
    publishers)
13 **EVENING STAR** (The East
    Anglian Daily Times Co.
    Limited, publishers)
13 **FELIXSTOWE TIMES (The**
    East Anglian Daily Times
    Co. Limited, publishers)
15 Smith Percy L. confctnr
17 Hooper T. Ridley, florist
17a, Hooper T. Ridley
19 Hills & Steele, universal stores
21 Jay's Furnishing Stores, house
    furnishers
23 Elmo Stores, grocers
25 Seager Rt. Ltd. ham curers
25a, Ranson Ernest C
    Ipswich Gas Light Co. (offices
    & showrooms)
29 Akester's Ltd. laundry (re-
    ceiving office). See advert
29a, Eade Miss R. K. ladies' hair-
    dresser
31 & 33 **WHILLIER'S MUSIC**
    STORES. See advertisement
35 Fieldings Ltd. cycle agts
35 Fields Gordon W

37 Smith Frank Frost, confctnr
39 Co-operative Society's Reading
    Room & Library
39 Barrett Wltr. Rt
39 & 41 Ipswich Industrial Co-
    operative Society Ltd. (hard-
    ware dept)
43 Cosser Whitfield & Lankesheer,
    photographers
45 Buckland C. & Son, florists
43a, Salutation P.H., E. C. Bloom-
    field
45a, 47 & 49 List Albert Ltd.
    domestic machinery wareho
...... here is Old Foundry rd ......
Sarony (Herbt. Seaman, propr.),
    photographers
Quick Service Boot Repairers (W.
    H. Broughall Ltd)

     South side.
2 & 4 Fifty Shilling Tailors
    (The) (Prices Tailors Ltd.
    proprs)
6 & 8 **SMALLEYS** (C. Smalley
    M.P.S., F.S.M.C., F.I.O.,
    F.B.O.A. propr.), chemists
    & opticians. Tel. No. Ipswich
    2307. See advertisement
10, 12, 14 & 16 Sunnucks Ltd. out-
    fitters
18 Sennitts, provsn. mers
20 Shelley Ann, costumier
........here is Cross Keys la. ....
    Woolworth F. W. & Co. Ltd.
    bazaar
32 Pilcher & Chittenden, fruitrs
32a, Dewhurst J. H. Ltd. butchers
34 & 34a, Curry's Ltd. cycle dlrs
36 Millett E. G. & Co. Ltd. out-
    fitters
38 to 66 **IPSWICH INDUS-**
    TRIAL CO-OPERATIVE
    SOCIETY LTD. (C. R.
    Caselton, managing secre-
    tary). T N 2154
.... here is Cox la ....
68 Shelbourne Geo. B. newsagt
68a, **HANTON & SMITH,** general
    & motor & brass & aluminium
    founders. Telephone 2632.
    See advertisement
70 Beehive P.H. Tom R. Beckerleg

50. Extract from a directory: from Kelly's *Directory of Ipswich* (1939),
p. 65, covering Carr Street, Ipswich.

This development in shops and shopping, 'The Retailing Revolution', provides an excellent organisational and conceptual framework for a local study. Students could be given a run of directories, and asked to note all examples of 'Companies', 'Limited Companies' and 'Wholesalers' as they appeared. For instance, in 1881 the only large company in Carr Street was the Ipswich Industrial Co-operative Society, but by 1894 the Danish Dairy Company, The Eastern Counties Dairy Institute Limited and the Ipswich Gas Light Company had arrived. By 1910, 10 such establishments had appeared in the street, and by 1939, 16 (Woolworths came in the early 1920s). At the present day, the dominance of such outlets is almost total.

Changes in the use and occupancy of particular sites are also worth studying. No. 52 Carr Street was occupied by a bootmaker in 1881, by a tailor and outfitter in 1885, by a fish merchant in 1890 and by a fancy draper in 1894. By 1910 the site had been incorporated into the premises of the Co-op. According to the directory of 1881, No. 60 Carr Street was vacant. In 1885, though, it was occupied by a pork butcher and by Baker & Co., London Supply Company; in 1890 by Baker & Raynham, Tea Dealers, Grocers and Provision Merchants (a partnership?) and by the pork butcher. In 1894 the pork butcher, George Norton, was still there, but George Baldwin's dairy had taken over the other shop. By 1910 the site had again completely changed hands, and was occupied by a warehouse for domestic machinery and by a general and fancy draper. By the 1920s this site, too, had been absorbed by the Co-op. On the other hand, some shops have survived over most, or even all, of the period under study.

A satisfactory assignment for the study of a shopping street could be based on directories alone, but it would undoubtedly be improved by weaving in other sources such as photographs of shop-fronts and advertisements.

Architecture in the street: a changing townscape

It is worth repeating that, when a main street is being investigated, students should visit it at an early stage, and be encouraged to study and record its standing buildings and other physical features. They will quickly realise that the most important earlier evidence is likely to survive above the level of ground-floors, above the plate glass and plastic of modern shop-fronts. Different styles, building materials, roof-lines and ornamentation, as well as those invaluable plaques which bear dates or initials to commemorate new building or re-modelling, should be carefully noted in words, drawings and photographs.

Other kinds of visual evidence may well exist in some quantity, and give excellent opportunities for studying the changing physical environment: photographs, drawings, panoramas, maps and plans. To those can be added the verbal evidence of guide books, newspapers, advertisements, street directories and local pamphlets.

To illustrate something of the potential for this kind of study, this section reproduces examples of the evidence which exists for Carr Street in Ipswich. Each different kind of surviving evidence is sampled, accompanied by notes which draw attention to the most important historical clues [51-60]. These materials, together with other bits of evidence mentioned earlier in the text (for instance, the photograph [**3**], the drawings of the Co-operative Society's building [**41**], the sample of the town plan [**37**] and the reminiscences of Mr. Tibbenham [**43**]) could be used as a pack for a classroom exercise. They could lead to a piece of writing based on the questions listed on p. 44.

51. Historical photograph, 1881: showing the junction of Carr Street and Upper Brook Street, Ipswich. Taken from the work of a local photographer, William Vick, and published in his *Ipswich Past and Present* (1888). The view shows a row of typical timber-framed buildings of the 16th or 17th centuries with overhanging first floors, beneath which later shop-fronts have been inserted. This is good evidence that the architecture of this part of the street was still largely 'vernacular' and unaltered at the beginning of the decade. For a dramatic contrast, *see* [**54**].

52. Historical photograph, undated: showing a fine timber-framed building on the corner of Cox Lane and Carr Street, Ipswich (Suffolk Photographic Survey, Suffolk Record Office). The building appears to be unoccupied. Note the details of the structure: the close studding of the frame, the elaborately carved corner-post, and the shallow arches over windows and doors. Are there any clues as to the photograph's date, for example, in the dress of the by-standers or in the poster on the right? The building glimpsed to the right is the Co-op store of 1886 [**41**], so the photograph certainly post-dates that. Note also Mr. Tibbenham's reference to this timber-framed building being sold off 'in later years' [**43**], and the panorama of the Co-op buildings [**58**] which shows this site as having been developed by 1908.

53. Newspaper article referring to demolition of an old building: an extract from the *East Anglian Daily Times*, 30 September 1957, referring to the demolition, fifty years previously, of the house depicted above [**52**]. If the photograph does show the building empty, then it may well have been taken just before the demolition. The newspaper article shows clearly that the house was demolished within three weeks of its sale, hence in the autumn of 1907. The fourth paragraph uses architectural terms which students should explore and explain. This is a good example of the wealth of information buried in newspaper files, and sometimes found quite fortuitously.

TUDOR HOUSE DISAPPEARS

Fifty years ago this week, when nostalgia about the "Old Ipswich" that was disappearing was just as strong as it is to-day, a Tudor house at the corner of Carr Street and Cox Lane was sold by auction for £75.

The site had just been acquired by Ipswich Co-operative Society, who at present have their main Ipswich premises around it. The house was sold with the condition that it was pulled down in 21 days

The building, which had been renovated in 1890, had the second finest corner post in the town—the best being still in existence at the corner of St. Nicholas Street and Silent Street.

It was richly panelled with sunk tracery below the cap, and the bracket above the cap had similar tracery, the spandrels being carved with Gothic floriations. The cap had a cresting of Tudor flower ornament and beneath the abascus was a hollow cusped soffit. The lower part had been cut away and a stone base inserted.

Inside the three-storey building the rooms were a complicated catacomb that brought to mind Mr. Pickwick's muddle with rooms' at another Ipswich premises the Great White Horse Hotel. The two upper floors each had seven rooms, all opening into each other and approached by two extremely narrow and angular staircases.

The auctioneer at the sale, Mr. Herbert Wright, said he was sorry to see the house go, but he supposed it was inevitable. The first bid showed the scepticism of the business mind on matters of culture. It was for £5.

Then came a serious bid for £30. The bidding hung fire for a long time after that and finally the auctioneer knocked the house down at £75 to Mr. Harris, a builder.

CARR STREET

Is the continuation of Tavern Street, and the main line of communication between the Cornhill and St. Helen's, including the County Hall and Assize Courts; it was for many years the subject of severe comment owing to its narrowness; till in 1887 a Company was formed called the "Carr Street Improvement Company, Limited," with the object of widening this important thoroughfare. Many of the leading inhabitants supported the scheme, and about £5,000 was raised in share capital, while the corporation granted a subsidy of £3,500, and about £17,000 was raised on mortgage; the £25,000 thus raised has been expended on the pulling down on the South side of the street a row of dingy old houses from Brook Street to the Old House, setting back the frontage line and erecting handsome red brick shops and dwelling houses; and on the North side demolishing the whole of the old buildings between the *East Anglian Daily Times* Office and Major's Corner.⸵ The land on this side is now being gradually covered with new and more convenient premises, amongst those in contemplation being a large building as a Working Girls' Club and Home, and a handsome New Theatre with all the modern appliances. By these alterations the width of the street has been increased in the narrowest part from 19 ft. to 32 ft., and the mean width from 23½ ft. to 30½ ft. Although not a financial success, the company may be congratulated on having achieved one of the greatest street improvements in Ipswich.

54. Historical photograph of 1890: showing the junction of Carr Street and Upper Brook Street, Ipswich, from William Vick's *Ipswich Past and Present* (1890). This photograph is taken from exactly the same place as [**51**], but the scene has been totally transformed in the intervening two years. Note that the new development is all of a piece, that the new buildings are much higher than the old, and that the new materials are red and white brick instead of timber and plaster.

55. Extract from an early guidebook: taken from Pawsey & Hayes, *Illustrated Guide to Ipswich* (1890), p. 43. This is a major piece of evidence for the transformation of Carr Street in the late 1880s. It gives information on the origin of a development company, describes where changes were happening, and specifies new buildings and the widening of the street.

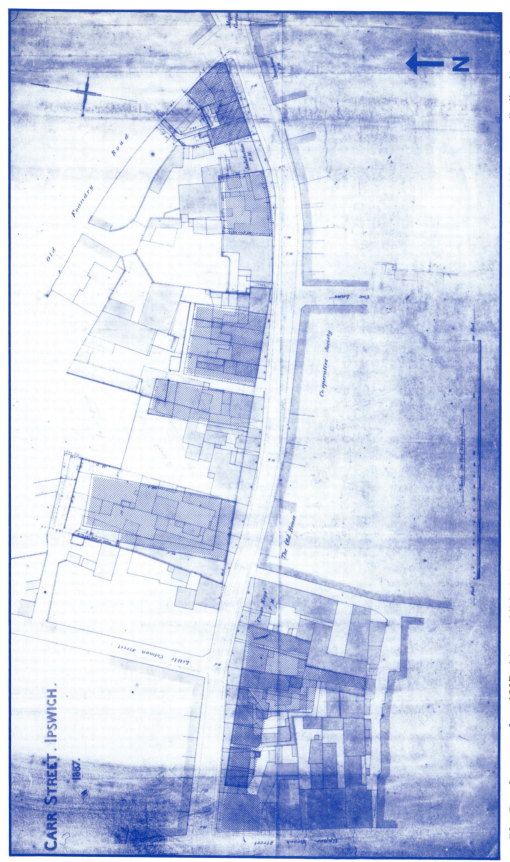

56. Development plan, 1887: this unpublished plan must have been prepared by the development company which in the 1880s was radically changing Carr Street, Ipswich. Notice the widening of the street, the moving back of frontages on both sides, and the identification by numbers of those properties which are affected.

22 Manning William
24 Whittle Harry
26 Moye James Bishop

Here is Sedan Street.

Here is Quadling Street.

40 Lamb Thomas Woodward
42 Durrant Adin Thomas
44 Pratt David
46 Sparkes Henry James
48 Snowden Francis Broom
50 Sharman Robert
52 Gardiner Frederick
54 Daldry David
56 Hughes Charles
58 Turvey Joseph
60 Lingwood Leonard
62 Colchester Brewery Company's Stores
64 "Suffolk" Hotel—Blowers Wm., Victuallor, see also Commercial Road

Here is Commercial Road.

CARR STREET.

From Tavern Street, Northgate Street, and Upper Brook Street to St. Margaret's Street, St. Helen's Street, and Upper Orwell Street.

LEFT HAND.

1 & 3 Unoccupied
5 Cook James Wells, Wholesale and Retail Confectioner, and at 18, Tacket Street; Steam Works — 27, Foundation Street
7 Aldous Edward, London and Paris Hat Warehouseman, Men's Mercer, Hosier, Glover, &c.
9 Andrews Herbert Walter
Andrews Mrs. Herbert Walter, Dress and Mantle Maker
11 Howe Thomas Potter, M.C.P.

Here is Little Colman Street.

Carr Street continued.

13 Printing and Publishing Offices of *East Anglian Daily Times*, Publisher, Frederick William Wilson; *Star of the East* (every evening), Publisher, Thomas Richards Elkington, *Suffolk Times and Mercury* (Friday), Publisher, George Manby
15 Ward Joseph, Family, Naval and Military Tailor, and Woollen Draper
Building Sites
29 Stiles Edwin, Baker, Confectioner, and Pastry Cook.—Refreshment Rooms
31 Laurence and Scott (Limited), Electrical Engineers. Local Manager—Wm. B. Sisling. Head Office and Works—Gothic Works, Norwich
33 Banks Harry, Tobacconist
35 Jackson Edward, Ticket Writer, Toy and Fancy Repository
37 Kitton Charles H., Fancy Draper
41 Unoccupied
Building Sites.
49 & 51 "Salutation" Inn—Last — Victualler
Building Sites.

Here is Old Foundry Road.

61 Butcher Frederick, Currier, Leather Merchant, & Upper and Grindery Dealer; and at Debenham

Here are St. Margaret's Street and St Helen's Street.

RIGHT HAND.

2 & 4 Pick George Thomas, General Draper, Victoria House, see also 1 & 8, Upper Brook Street
6 Brereton Hy. Arthur, Fruiterer and Waiter
8 Eastern Counties Dairy Institute Limited, (Manager—George Berry) and at Akenham
Berry George

10 Candler James Fredk., Watchmaker, Jeweller, Silversmith, and Optician
12 Cossey James Davis, Chemist and Druggist
14 Chilver Mrs. Susan, Berlin Wool, Art Needlework, and Fancy Emporium, Stationer, &c.
16 Unoccupied
18 Scheuermann George, Butcher, and Ham and Bacon Curer
20 Unoccupied
26 & 28 "Cross Keys" Commercial Hotel — Frederick Makin, Proprietor
30 Casley Reginald Kennedy, M.D., Surgeon
32 Gooding and Hill, Solicitors
Gooding Samuel (firm Gooding and Hill) Solicitor and Commissioner for Oaths. Clerk to Guardians of Bosmero and Claydon Union.
Hill Leonard (firm Gooding and Hill) Solicitor
Sleigh Samuel
34 Tibbenham John, Carver, Gilder, Picture Frame Maker, and Artists' Material Dealer
36 Fisher Charles, Hairdresser and Tobacconist
38 to 42 Ipswich Industrial Cooperative Society Limited (Central Stores)

Here is Cox Lane.

48 Withers William Richard, Muffin Baker and Confectioner
50 Greengrass Frederick George, News Agent and Confectioner
52 Pratt John, Fish Merchant
54 Greatrex Frederick, Collar Maker and Saddler
56 Barber Shearman, Baker, Dairyman, and Poulterer
51 Butters Charles Edward, Hairdresser and Perfumer
60 Baker and Raynham, Tea Dealers, Grocers, and Provision Merchants
Raynham Arthur
60A Norton George, Pork Butcher, Poulterer, and Dairyman

Carr Street continued.

see Tavern Street
Fish (F.) and Son's Manufactory
64 "Race Horse"—Wheeler John W., Beer Retailer
66 Dixey George, Arthur, and Sophia, Wholesale and Retail Fish Merchants, and at 9, King Street
Dixey Arthur
68 Kerridge Miss Emma, Confectioner
70 "Shoulder of Mutton and Round of Beef "—Maddocks Thos., Beer and Wine Retailer
72 Maddocks Thomas, Dining and Refreshment Rooms
74 Mason William Carrington, Wholesale and Retail Butcher

Here are St. Helen's and Upper Orwell Streets.

CASTLE STREET.

From Stirling Street to Perth Street.

LEFT HAND.

1 Powell Mrs. F., General Shopkeeper
3 Poole Charles
5 to 31 Small Tenements

Here is Perth Street.

RIGHT HAND.

Saunders Mrs. Elizabeth, Beer Retailer

Here is Perth Street.

CAULDWELL AVENUE.

From Woodbridge Road to Tovell's Road.

LEFT HAND.

Dunnett O., Dairyman, Victoria Dairy
Carringood William, Avenue Villa
Mayhew James, Jobbing Gardener, Brundish Villa

57. **Extract from a directory during redevelopment**: Kelly's *Directory of Ipswich* (1890), pp. 108-10, mentions several 'building sites' in Carr Street, which must refer to the activities of the development company, and two 'unoccupied' sites which were presumably awaiting their new occupants. This is very useful evidence of development and rebuilding in progress.

PANORAMIC VIEW OF CENTRAL PREMISES, CARR STREET, IPSWICH

WITH DATES OF ERECTION OF THE VARIOUS BUILDINGS.

1913	1928	1908		1886
CENTRAL GROCERY AND TEAROOM.	NEW BOOT AND SHOE AND FURNISHING DEPARTMENTS	CENTRAL DRAPERY	COX LANE	OUTFITTING DEPARTMENT, OFFICES AND HALLS ON 1ST AND 2ND FLOORS.

Since this view was prepared, additional premises on the left of the Central Grocery have been purchased, and will accommodate

CHEMISTS', and LADIES' and GENTS' HAIRDRESSING DEPARTMENTS

58. A photographic panorama, 1928: this shows all the premises of the Ipswich Co-operative Society in Carr Street, and is taken from a booklet on the history of the Society. Notice in particular the different architectural styles with their respective dates. The first 20th-century block of 1908 still has its date emblazoned on the actual structure, with the motto 'Each for All and All for Each'. The caption reveals that yet another property had been recently acquired, to the left of the panorama, for a chemist's shop and a hairdressing department. When compared with the photograph of 1989 [**3**], this panorama shows the need for modern students to look above ground-floor level to appreciate the character of standing buildings.

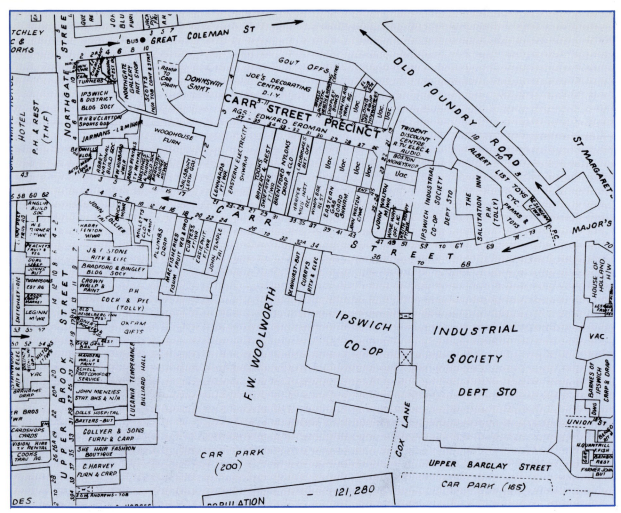

59. Shopping centre plan, 1973: one of a useful series published nationally by Charles E. Goad Ltd. This plan of Ipswich, when compared with the town plan of 1881, shows how the Co-operative Society has come to dominate the south side of Carr Street, while a major redevelopment of the 1960s — the Carr Street Precinct — now dominates the north side. Apart from the Co-op, the one building which still retains the use it had in 1881 is the *Salutation Inn*.

60. Modern photograph, 1989: showing a large shopping precinct built in the 1960s on the north side of Carr Street, Ipswich. Such 'comprehensive redevelopment' can be paralleled in the shopping centres of many English towns, and raises fascinating questions about modern planning, urban design and conservation. This Carr Street precinct of the 1960s compares interestingly with the work of the development company of 1887; together they represent the two most important periods of change in the architectural character of the street. When, incidentally, does a modern photograph become historical? Should we not take photographs as a deliberate historical record?

V

THE YOUNG HISTORIAN

At all stages of their work, students must be encouraged to examine evidence critically, to correlate their sources and to analyse them in response to specific questions and problems. This work of 'detection' is something which the teacher should reinforce as often as possible, since it is the essence of historical research. The students' conclusions, their final product, will need to be written in the same way. The aim is to produce a piece of original history which is a reasoned and critical discussion, supported by references carefully citing the evidence on which it is based.

Case studies

Higgs, E., 'Women, Occupations and Work in the 19th Century', *History Workshop Journal*, No. 23 (Spring 1987), pp. 59-80

Lee, J., 'Cherry Orchard: the growth of a Victorian Suburb', in Trinder, B. (ed.), *Victorian Shrewsbury* (Shropshire Libraries, 1984), pp. 114-29

Ravensdale, J. R., *History on Your Doorstep*, Ch. 2, 'Ealing: the History of a House', (BBC, 1982)

Redfern, J. B., 'Elite Surburbians: Early Victorian Edgbaston', *The Local Historian*, Vol. 15, No. 5 (1983), pp. 259-71

Sill, M., 'Mid-Nineteenth Century Labour Mobility: the Case of the Coal Miners of Hutton le Hole, Co. Durham', *Local Population Studies*, No. 22 (1979), pp. 44-50

INDEX

Note: References in **bold** refer to pages on which illustrations or documents appear.

advertisements, **54**, **55**, **56**; business, 49; in newspapers and directories, 56-7; shop, 59

age, in census returns, 11, 13

age structure, 19, 21, 23; tabulating, **22**

almanacks *see* directories

architects' drawings *see* drawings

architecture, **2**; changes in, 3, 44; of streets, 59-60; visual evidence of buildings, 1, 3

Artizans' and Labourers' Dwellings Improvement Acts (1875) (Cross's Acts), 37, 38

autobiographies, **25**

'biographies' of households, 41-2, 48-9, 51

birthplaces, 11, 13, 23, 25-6; of children, 23, 25; recording, **22**

Booth, Charles, social scientist, 41-2

boundaries, from rate books, 16

buildings *see* architecture

burial registers, used for 'biographies', 41-2

businesses: company, 44; family, 44; listed in directories, 59

census returns, 1, 11, 13, **30**; directions to enumerators, 11, **12**; and discrepancies, 46; and reconstructed maps, **7**; recording of households, 17-18, **18**; use of computers, 18; used for 'biographies', 41-2, 51; used for 'repopulation', 34, 51, *see also* enumerators, enumerators' books

chapels, 5, 42

churches, 5

Common Lodging Houses Act, 37

companies *see* businesses

computers, use of, 18

Co-operative Societies, 49, 51, 57

County Record Office, 1, 51

demographic trends, from census returns, 11

development and rebuilding, 1, 3, 49, **63**, **64**

directories, 13, **14**, 16, **47**, **58**; and changes in shops, 57; and street numbering, 46; used for 'repopulation', 34

discrepancies in documents, 37, 46

documentary sources, 1; use of, 5

documents: as evidence of changes in townscape, 44; facsimiles, 11, 13; transcription, 1, 17-18

drawings: architects', **4**, 49, **50**; as visual evidence, 59, 60

economic changes, evidence of, 44

enumerators: of census returns, 11, **12**, 13; mistakes by, 11, 13, 37

enumerators' books, **10**, **24**, **35**, **48**; household information from, 17-18; and street numbering, 46, 48

evidence: interpretation of, 19, 34, 44, 46, 67; recording, 3, 17-18

facsimiles, use of, 11

family history societies, 1

family planning, from analysis of households, 23

gardens, 32, 34

guide books, 59, **62**

health *see* public health; sanitation

households: analysis of, 48-9; in censuses and directories, 11, 13; size of, 19, 21

housing, 32, 34, 37; conditions, 5; improved, 23; and public health legislation, 37; slum clearance, 1, 5, **8**, 37; types of, 5, 32; from plans, 34

industrial sites, 5, **7**, 44

labour, migrant, 23; *see also* lodgers and lodging-houses; mobility

legislation, on sanitation, 37, 38-9

letters, **31**

libraries, 1, 51

life expectancy, 23

literacy, in census returns, 13

local authorities, 19th-century committees, 38-9

local history library, 1

local history societies, 1

lodgers and lodging-houses, 23, 24, 37

magazines, reminiscences in, 51-2
maps, 3, 5, **6**, **7**; Ordnance Survey, 3, 5, **8**; as
    visual evidence, 59, *see also* plans; town plans
Medical Officer of Health, annual reports, 37
microfilm, census returns on, 1
migration *see* lodgers and lodging-houses;
    mobility
mobility: evidence from birthplaces, 23, 25, 26;
    evidence from rate books, 26
museums: information about trades, 28;
    photographs and prints in, 3

newspapers, 59, **61**; advertisements in, 56-7;
    contemporary descriptions in, 49, **50**; court
    reports in, 41-2
Nuisances Removal Committee, 37, 39

occupations: analysis of, 29, 31; categories of, 29;
    in census returns, 11; female, 29, 31-2;
    seasonal and casual, 32; in shopping street,
    44; in street directories, 13, 16; unfamiliar,
    27-9
Office of Population Census and Surveys:
    returns, 11, 21, *see also* census returns
oral sources *see* reminiscences
overcrowding, 37, 40; in lodging-houses, 37
Overseers of the Poor: organised early census
    returns, 11; rate books of, 16
ownership of property, 16, 34, 49

pamphlets, 59; commemorative, 49, 51
photographs, 1, 49, **60**, **61**, **62**; of buildings, 3;
    modern, **66**; panoramas, **65**; of shops, 59
plans: development, **63**; of shopping centre, **66**
plaques, on buildings, 59
Poor Law Amendment Act, 16
Poor Law Unions, 11
poor-rate books, **15**, 16; *see also* rate books
population: and age structure, 21, 23; and
    household size, 21; of shopping street, 44
poverty, cycle of, 42-3
printed sources: commemorative histories, 51;
    contemporary descriptions, **28**, **40**, **44**;
    dictionaries, 27, 28; historical studies, **26**, **27**;
    local histories, 1
prints, architectural, 3, **4**
public health, 38-9, 40; medical officer of, 37;
    standards of, 23
Public Health Act (1875), 39
Public Health Committee, 37, 38-9
public houses, 5, 42
rate books, 16, **36**, **48**; compared with census

returns, 26; and discrepancies, 46, 48; used
    for 'biographies', 41-2; used for
    'repopulation', 34
rebuilding and development, **63**, **64**
record office *see* County Record Office
recording information *see* evidence, recording
reference library, 1
registers of deaths, as source for public health,
    37
Registrar General, and census returns, 11
reminiscences, 1, 49, 51-3, **52**, 60
'repopulation' of streets, 34, 37; evidence from
    commemorative histories for, 51
'retailing revolution', 59
Rowntree, Seebohm, social scientist, 42

sanitation, 34, 38-9; drainage, 5, 37, 40;
    inspectors' reports, 37, **37**, **38-9**; legislation
    on, 37, 38-9; ventilation, 34, 37, 40; water
    supply, 37, 40
shops: changes in ownership and occupancy, 57,
    59; co-operative, 49, 51, 57; national
    retailers, 57; private local, 57; reminiscences
    of, 51-2; study of, 44, 46; visual evidence of, 3
street directories *see* directories
street furniture, 5, 59
street names, 5
street numbering, from directories, 46
street trades, 52-3
streets, shopping, study of, 44, 46
Sunday schools, 42
surnames: occupational, 29; spelling variations,
    37

town plans, 5, **9**, **20**, **33**, **45**, 46, 59, 60;
    limitations for 'repopulation', 34, *see also*
    maps; plans
townscape *see* architecture
trades *see* occupations

urban growth, 5
Urban Sanitary Authorities, 37, 38

vice and virtue, 42
visual evidence: architecture, 1, 3, 44, 59-60; *see
    also* drawings; maps; photographs
wholesalers, listed in directories, 59
women, occupations of, 31-2
work *see* occupations
Working Men's Institute, 42
writers, local, 37